D1092184

POSTSCRIPTS

BY J. B. PRIESTLEY

FICTION

PLAYS

MISCELLANEOUS

POSTSCRIPTS

BY

J. B. PRIESTLEY

WILLIAM HEINEMANN LTD

LONDON :: TORONTO

FIRST PUBLISHED 1940

PRINTED IN GREAT BRITAIN AT THE WINDMILL PRESS
KINGSWOOD, SURREY

PREFACE

One of the oldest and stalest devices of book-making is to suggest that you would never have published the thing at all if you had not been entreated to do so by your friends and admirers. (And who was the well-known reviewer who said that when he encountered this statement at the beginning of a new book, he always sent out for his cudgel?) But here for once this is nothing more nor less than the exact truth. It was never my intention to publish the following talks, which were meant to be spoken and heard over the air and not to be read in cold print. They are wireless talks and not essays. And I have left them exactly as they were, without a speck of re-touching. If I had had my way they would never have re-appeared in this form, to be examined at leisure instead of being caught on the wing every Sunday at nine-fifteen, but the requests for a volume of them have come in so thick and fast during these last three months, that I felt it would be churlish to refuse. So here they are, and please don't blame me if you should change your mind about them now, for they have already done the work they were intended to do.

Two important conclusions emerge from my experience of broadcasting these Postscripts. The first, and less

important, is the immense, the staggering power and
effect of broadcasting. I have been hard at it getting
through to the public mind, in one way or another, for
about twenty years, but as a medium of communication
this broadcasting makes everything else seem like the
method of a secret society. So long as you don't go on
too long and the listeners are not tired of you, a mere
whisper over the air seems to start an avalanche.
Mention a couple of ducks, and they are photographed
as if they were film stars. Refer to a pie in a shop
window, and instantly there are pilgrimages to it.
Unfortunately the only persons here who do not seem
aware of this terrific power of the broadcast word are
the members of our War Cabinet, who still do not realise
that in the B.B.C. we have something as important to
us in this war, which is quite unlike previous wars, as
an army or navy or air force. The official under-valua-
tion of this great medium of communication and per-
suasion is to my mind one of the most serious weaknesses
of our war effort.

(And here, as a temporary colleague, I must add a
word of praise for the whole staff of the B.B.C., for in
my opinion during these last six months these men,
women and girls—controllers, producers, announcers,
engineers, secretaries—have done a grand job, a much
better one than most members of the listening public are
yet able to realise. They have kept going, working almost
to a punctual second, through the worst raids, and have
collectively and individually faced and overcome difficulties and, at times, dangers about which as yet the
public knows nothing. I trust that readers will take my

word for this, and I can only hope that somebody is writing the whole story.)

The second and more important conclusion that emerges from this short chapter of broadcasting experience is that the British listening public as a whole, and that means a gigantic cross-section of all our people, responds immediately to any sincere attempt to use a little insight and to penetrate beneath the surface of this conflict. The tricks of the writing trade and some fortunate accidents of voice and manner are all very well, but what really holds the attention of most decent folk is a genuine sharing of feelings and views on the part of the broadcaster. He must talk as if he were among serious friends, and not as if he had suddenly been appointed head of an infants' school. People may be almost inarticulate themselves and yet recognise in an instant when something that is at least trying to be real and true is being said to them. Thus it is useless handing out to most of them a lot of dope left over from the last war. They may not understand this present war, but unlike many official persons, they do know that it is not the last war, that a simple, almost idiotic nationalism will not do, that either we are fighting to bring a better world into existence or we are merely assisting at the destruction of such civilisation as we possess.

A final word. Many listeners, writing appreciative letters to which I am sorry I have never had time to reply, seem to have imagined from certain remarks of mine that most of my correspondents have been hostile and abusive. I apologise—if it was my fault—for conveying this impression, for the truth is that of the thousands of letters that these Postscripts brought me, only a very tiny minority were anything but warmly appreciative. And even most of these appeared to be in such a hurry to denounce what I said that they had not time to listen to what I said. But here—far removed from the proper time and place and method—is what I actually did say, upstairs and downstairs in Broadcasting House and elsewhere, Sunday after Sunday, during those strange months when first the world wondered if each week would see the end of us, then afterwards drew a long breath of relief and admiration, as the common folk of this island rose to meet the challenge and not only saved what we have that is good but began to dream of something much better.

J.B.P.

Wednesday, 5th June, 1940

I WONDER how many of you feel as I do about this great Battle and evacuation of Dunkirk. The news of it came as a series of surprises and shocks, followed by equally astonishing new waves of hope. It was all, from beginning to end, unexpected. And yet now that it's over, and we can look back on it, doesn't it seem to you to have an inevitable air about it—as if we had turned a page in the history of Britain and seen a chapter headed "Dunkirk" —and perhaps seen too a picture of the troops on the beach waiting to embark?

And now that this whole action is completed, we notice that it has a definite shape, and a certain definite character. What strikes me about it is how typically English it is. Nothing, I feel, could be more English than this Battle of Dunkirk, both in its beginning and its end, its folly and its grandeur. It was very English in what was sadly wrong with it; this much has been freely admitted, and we are assured will be freely discussed when the proper moment arrives. We have gone sadly wrong like this before; and here and now we must resolve never, never to do it again. Another such blunder may *not* be forgiven us.

But having admitted this much, let's do ourselves the

1

justice of admitting too that this Dunkirk affair was also very English (and when I say "English" I really mean British) in the way in which, when apparently all was lost, so much was gloriously retrieved. Bright honour was almost "plucked from the moon". What began as a miserable blunder, a catalogue of misfortunes and mis-calculations, ended as an epic of gallantry. We have a queer habit—and you can see it running through our history—of conjuring up such transformations. Out of a black gulf of humiliation and despair, rises a sun of blazing glory. This is not the German way. They don't make such mistakes (a grim fact that we should bear in mind) but also—they don't achieve such epics. There is never anything to inspire a man either in their victories or their defeats; boastful when they're winning, quick to whine when threatened with defeat—there is nothing about them that ever catches the world's imagination. That vast machine of theirs can't create a glimmer of that poetry of action which distinguishes war from mass murder. It's a machine—and therefore has no soul.

But here at Dunkirk is another English epic. And to my mind what was most characteristically English about it—so typical of us, so absurd and yet so grand and gallant that you hardly know whether to laugh or to cry when you read about them—was the part played in the difficult and dangerous embarkation—not by the war-ships, magnificent though they were—but by the little pleasure-steamers. We've known them and laughed at them, these fussy little steamers, all our lives. We have called them "the shilling sicks." We have watched them load and unload their crowds of holiday passengers—the gents full of high spirits and bottled beer, the ladies eating pork pies, the children sticky with peppermint rock. Sometimes they only went as far as the next seaside resort. But the boldest of them might manage a Channel crossing, to let everybody have a glimpse of Boulogne. They were usually paddle steamers, making a great deal more fuss with all their churning than they made speed; and they weren't proud, for they let you see their works going round. They liked to call themselves "Queens" and "Belles"; and even if they were new, there was always something old-fashioned, a Dickens touch, a mid-Victorian air, about them. They seemed to belong to the same ridiculous holiday world as pierrots and piers, sand castles, ham-and-egg teas, palmists, automatic machines, and crowded sweating promenades. But they were called out of that world—and, let it be noted—they were called out in good time and good order. Yes, these "Brighton Belles" and "Brighton Queens" left that innocent foolish world of theirs—to sail into the inferno, to defy bombs, shells, magnetic mines, torpedoes, machine-gun fire—to rescue our soldiers. Some of them—alas—will never return. Among those paddle steamers that will never return was one that I knew well, for it was the pride of our ferry service to the Isle of Wight—none other than the good ship "Gracie Fields". I tell you, we were proud of the "Gracie Fields", for she was the glittering queen of our local line, and instead of taking an hour over her voyage, used to do it, churning like mad, in forty-five minutes. And now never again will we board her at Cowes and go down into her dining saloon for a fine breakfast of bacon and eggs. She has paddled and churned away—for ever. But now—look—this little steamer, like all her brave and battered sisters, is immortal. She'll go sailing proudly down the years in the epic of Dunkirk. And our great grand-children, when they learn how we began this War by snatching glory out of defeat, and then swept on to victory, may also learn how the little holiday steamers made an excursion to hell and came back glorious.

Sunday, 9th June, 1940

I DON'T think there has ever been a lovelier English spring than this last one, now melting into full summer. Sometimes, in between listening to the latest news of battle and destruction, or trying to write about them myself, I've gone out and stared at the red japonica or the cherry and almond blossom, so clear and exquisite against the moss-stained old wall—and have hardly been able to believe my eyes; I've just gaped and gaped like a bumpkin at a fair through all these weeks of spring. Never have I seen (at least, not since I grew up) such a golden white of buttercups and daisies in the meadows. I'll swear the very birds have sung this year as they never did before. Just outside my study, there are a couple of blackbirds who think they're still in the Garden of Eden. There's almost a kind of mockery in their fluting. I think most of us have often felt we simply couldn't believe our eyes and ears: either the War wasn't real, or this spring wasn't real. One of them must be a dream. I've looked out of my house in the country on these marvellous days of sun and blue air—and I could see the blaze and bloom of the Californian poppies and the roses in the garden; then the twinkling beaches and the stately nodding elms—and then, beyond, the lush fields and the round green hills dissolving into the hazy blue of the sky. And I've stared at all this—and I've remembered the terrible news of battle and destruction I'd just heard or read—and I've felt that one or the other couldn't be true.

Sometimes I've felt that I was really staring at a beautifully painted silk curtain; and that at any moment it might be torn apart—its flowers, trees and green hills vanishing like smoke, to reveal the old Flanders Front, trenches and bomb craters, ruined towns, a scarred countryside, a sky belching death, and the faces of murdered children.

I had to remind myself that the peaceful and lovely scene before me was the real truth; that it was there long before the Germans went mad, and will be there when that madness is only remembered as an old nightmare.

Tennyson might have been prophesying this German madness in the spring when he wrote:

> "The fields are fair beside them,
>   The chestnut towers in his bloom;
> But they—they feel the desire of the deep—
> Fallen, follow their doom."

But sometimes, too, I've felt that the unusual loveliness of our gardens and meadows and hills has come home to us because these things are, so to speak, staring at us—as you see so many women now staring at their soldier husbands, sweethearts, sons, just before the trains take them away. It's as if this English landscape said: "Look at me, as I am now in my beauty and fullness of joy, and do not forget." And when I feel this, I feel too a sudden and very sharp anger; for I remember then how this island is threatened and menaced; how perhaps at this very moment, thin-lipped and cold-eyed Nazi staff officers are planning, with that mixture of method and lunacy which is all their own, how to project on to this countryside of ours those half-doped crazy lads they call parachute troops. This land that is ours, that appeals to us now in all its beauty, is at this moment only just outside the reach of these self-tormenting schemers and their millions who are used as if they were not human beings but automata, robots, mere "things". They drop them from planes as if they were merely bombs with arms and legs. They send them swarming forward in battle as if they were not fellow-men but death-dealing dolls, manufactured in Goering's factories.

Yesterday morning I saw the Nazi film, "Baptism of Fire," which deals with the invasion and attempted destruction of Poland. Now this is the film that has been used as a "bogy-man" to frighten neutrals who are about to be "protected" by the Reich. We're told how it has been shown at various German embassies and how all who saw it sat silent and fearful. What is it really like? I'll tell you. It's the opposite of "The Lion Has Wings"— and I mean by that, that it presents all the contrary qualities. Our film didn't take itself too solemnly; showed our airmen as likeable human beings, cracking jokes with their wives and sweethearts. But this Nazi picture is all "drums and trombones"—gloom and threats. A loud German voice bullies you through it all. There's a lot about destruction and death, and not a

B

glimmer of humour, or fun, or ordinary human relation-ships. It's all machines and robot stuff. The key-word throughout is "Bomb." "Oh" (it says)—"Bogy, bogy!"

Well, I make no pretence of being a hero—but I'll say here and now that it didn't frighten *me*, or any of the other people who saw it yesterday morning. It left us where it found us. No, that's not quite true; for speaking for myself, it did seem extraordinarily interesting and revealing. What it plainly revealed were the habits of mind of the people who made it. It showed that they thought only in terms of Force and Fear. They con-sidered it a wonderful bogy-man because they them-selves are very susceptible to bogy-men. It was a characteristic product—in spite of considerable technical merits—of half-crazy, haunted, fearful minds; of a people who, for some reason best known to themselves, are ready to sacrifice liberty, scholarship, art, philosophy, and all the humanities, in order to turn themselves into a kind of overgrown species of warrior-ant.

And the rest of us have simply to stand up and say: "NO!" If we do that firmly, and cheerfully, and throw all our energy into the task of making that "No" decisive, these people are done for. The Nazis understand—and it is their great secret—all the contemptible qualities of men. They have a lightning eye for an opponent's weak-ness. But what they don't understand, because there's nothing in their nature or experience to tell them, is that men also have their hour of greatness, when weakness suddenly towers into strength; when ordinary easy-going tolerant men rise in their anger and strike down evil like the angels of the wrath of God.

Sunday, 16th June, 1940

A NIGHT or two ago, I had my first spell with our Local Defence Volunteers or "Parashots." I'd been on the muster for the previous fortnight—but I'd been away, busy with other work, so I hadn't been able to see how our village was keeping watch and ward. Ours is a small and scattered village, but we'd had a fine response to the call for Volunteers; practically every able-bodied man in the place takes his turn. The post is on top of a high down, with a fine view over a dozen wide parishes. The men I met up there the other night represented a good cross-section of English rural life; we had a parson, a bailiff, a builder, farmers and farm labourers. Even the rarer and fast disappearing rural trades were represented —for we had a hurdle-maker there; and his presence, together with that of a woodman and a shepherd, made me feel sometimes that I'd wandered into one of those rich chapters of Thomas Hardy's fiction in which his rustics meet in the gathering darkness on some Wessex hillside. And indeed there was something in the preliminary talk, before the sentries were posted for the night, that gave this whole horrible business of air raids and threatened invasion a rustic, homely, almost comfortable atmosphere, and really made a man feel

9

more cheerful about it. In their usual style, these country chaps called every aeroplane "she." They'd say: "Ay, she come along through the gap and over along by Little Witchett—as I see with me own eyes. Then searchloights picks her up—moight be Black Choine way or farther along, over boi Colonel Wilson's may be—an' Oi says to Tarm: 'Won't be long now, you'll see, afore they gets her'—and then, bingo, masters, down she comes!" They have the sound countryman's habit of relating everything intimately to their own familiar background. Now of course this doesn't take away any of the real menace, but what it does do is somehow to put all this raiding and threatened invasion in their proper places. The intellectual is apt to see these things as the lunatic end of everything, as part of a crazy Doomsday Eve, and so he goes about moaning, or runs away to America. But the simple and saner countryman sees this raiding and invading as the latest manifestation of that everlasting menace which he always has to fight— sudden blizzards at lambing time, or floods just before the harvest.

I think the countryman knows, without being told, that we hold our lives here, as we hold our farms, upon certain terms. One of those terms is that while wars still continue, while one nation is ready to hurl its armed men at another, you must if necessary stand up and fight for your own. And this decision comes from the natural piety of simple but sane men. Such men, you will notice, are happier now than the men who have lost that natural piety.

Well, as we talked on our post on the hilltop, we

watched the dusk deepen in the valleys below, where our
women-folk listened to the news as they knitted by the
hearth, and we remembered that these were our homes
and that now at any time they might be blazing ruins,
and that half-crazy German youths, in whose empty
eyes the idea of honour and glory seems to include every
form of beastliness, might soon be let loose down there.
The sentries took their posts. There was a mist coming
over the down. Nothing much happened for a time. A
green light that seemed to defy all black-out regulations
turned out to be merely an extra large and luminous
glow-worm; the glow-worms, poor ignorant little
creatures, don't know there's a war on and so continue
lighting themselves up. A few searchlights went stabbing
through the dusk and then faded. The mist thickened,
and below in all the valleys, there wasn't the faintest
glimmer of light. You heard the ceaseless high melancholy singing of the telegraph wires in the wind.

So we talked about what happened to us in the last
war, and about the hay and the barley, about beef and
milk and cheese and tobacco. Then a belt of fog over to
the left became almost silvery, because somewhere along
there all the searchlights were sweeping the sky. Then
somewhere behind that vague silveriness, there was a
sound as if gigantic doors were being slammed to. There
was the rapid stabbing noise of anti-aircraft batteries,
and far away some rapping of machine-guns. Then the
sirens went, in our two nearest towns, as if all that part of
the darkened countryside, like a vast trapped animal,
were screaming at us.

But then the sounds of bombs and gunfire and planes

all died away. The "All Clear" went, and then there was nothing but the misty cool night, drowned in silence, and this handful of us on the hilltop. I remember wishing then that we could send all our children out of this island, every boy and girl of them across the sea to the wide Dominions, and turn Britain into the greatest fortress the world has known; so that then, with an easy mind, we could fight and fight these Nazis until we broke their black hearts.

I felt too up there a powerful and rewarding sense of community; and with it too a feeling of deep continuity. There we were, ploughman and parson, shepherd and clerk, turning out at night, as our forefathers had often done before us, to keep watch and ward over the sleeping English hills and fields and homesteads. I've mentioned Thomas Hardy, whose centenary has just been celebrated. Don't you find in his tales and poems, often derived from the talk he listened to as a boy, a sense that Napoleon, with *his* threatened invasion by the Grand Army at Boulogne, was only just round the corner? And I felt, out in the night on the hilltop, that the watch they kept then was only yesterday; that all this raiding and threat of invasion, though menacing and dangerous enough, was not some horror big enough to split the world—but merely our particular testing time; what *we* must face, as our forefathers faced such things, in order to enjoy our own again. It would come down upon us; it would be terrible; but it would pass. You remember Hardy's song: "In Time of The Breaking of Nations":

"Only a man harrowing clods
  In a slow silent walk,
With an old horse that stumbles and nods,
  Half asleep as they stalk;

Only thin smoke without flame
  From the heaps of couch-grass:
Yet this will go onward the same
  Though Dynasties pass.

Yonder a maid and her wight
  Come whispering by;
War's annals will fade into night
  Ere their story die."

THE other night, here in London, I did something I hadn't done for many months—I went to a cinema. It was showing an American comic film, which I enjoyed for what it was worth; but when it had been running for about an hour I began to lose interest. Then I had for a moment that "something-unpleasant-coming" feeling which you wake up to on a morning when you've arranged to see your dentist. But I knew it was nothing like a dentist: what was it? And then, the next moment, it was as if a hand of ice were resting on my shoulder—I remembered that we were in the middle of this war, preparing to live on a giant fortress, and the Gestapo were in Paris.

I didn't find it easy after that to pay much attention to the film, and wasn't sorry when I found myself out in the cool fresh night sauntering home through the strange dreamlike streets of this wartime London. Having been taken away from the war—if only for an hour—by the nonsensical film, I seemed to come back to the war almost with a fresh mind, ready to dig down and examine its roots all over again. Or perhaps it would be truer to say, that as I walked home under an exquisite night sky that might be loaded with death, what I dug into and examined was my own mind.

Now ever since the faked "burning" of the Reichstag—
ever since that "week-end of the long knives," when
Hitler had so many of his associates murdered—I think
I have known that in the end it must come to this: that
there must come a night when I would find myself
walking through a blacked-out London in an England
that was being turned into a fortress.

I don't pretend to any notable consistency, but it's a
fact—and cold print can prove it—that about Hitler and
the Nazis I have always held the same opinion—the
opinion that they were evil, and that the time must come
when either we must destroy them or they would destroy
us; they were no more to be compromised with than
typhoid fever is to be compromised with. You might as
well try to come to an amicable settlement with a pack of
ravening wolves. My feeling from the first, I think, had
nothing to do with economics and politics, but was really
moral—or, if you like, religious. Here, in these cruel
figures who emerged from the underworld, who promptly
destroyed the cultural life of their country, turned
workers into serfs again, trained boys to be brutes,
brushed away the last specks of honour, organised two
vast new government departments—one for systematic
lying, the other for equally systematic torture; and even
perverted and poisoned the life of the family, so that
school children became police spies at the very dinner
table—here, I say, was something that cut deeper than
the economic disagreements and political differences.

Here, I felt, was the growing corruption, the darkening
despair of our modern world, shaping itself into one vast
dark face—a German dark face, that would call to other

dark faces elsewhere. Every nation has two faces—a
bright face and a dark face. I had always been ready to
love the bright face of Germany which speaks to us of
beautiful music, profound philosophy, Gothic romance,
young men and maidens wandering through the
enchanted forests. I had been to Germany before the
last war, walking from one little inn to another in the
Rhineland. After the war I went back, and wrote in
praise of the noble Rhine, the wet lilac and the rust-
coloured Castle of Heidelberg, the carpets of flowers and
the ice-green torrents of the Bavarian Alps. But after the
Nazis came, I went no more. The bright face had gone,
and in its place was the vast dark face with its broken
promises and endless deceit, its swaggering Storm
Troopers and dreaded Gestapo, its bloodstained basements where youths were hardened by the torture of
decent elderly folk—the terror and the shame, not just
their shame, but our shame, the shame of the whole
watching world, of the concentration camps.

I knew that wherever these over-ambitious, ruthless,
neurotic men took their power, security and peace and
happiness would vanish. Unhappy themselves—for what
they are can be read in their faces, and plainly heard in
their barking or screaming voices—they wish to spread
their unhappiness everywhere. And I believed then—
and am convinced now—that if the world had not been
half-rotten, over-cynical, despairing, it would have risen
at once in its wrath before the great terror machine was
completed, and sent these evil men and their young
bullies back to their obscure corners, the back rooms of
beer-houses, and cellars, out of which they crept to try

and bring the whole world down to their own dreary back-room gangster level.

Many people are mystified by the existence of so many "fifth columnists" who are ready to work for Nazi-ism outside Germany; but, you see, Nazi-ism is not really a political philosophy, but an attitude of mind—the expression in political life of a certain very unpleasant temperament—of the man who hates Democracy, reasonable argument, tolerance, patience and humorous equality—the man who loves bluster and swagger uniforms and bodyguards and fast cars, plotting in back rooms, shouting and bullying, taking it out of all the people who have made him feel inferior. It's not really a balanced, grown-up attitude of mind at all: it belongs to people who can't find their way out of their adolescence, who remain overgrown, tormenting, cruel schoolboys— middle-aged "dead end kids". That's why the gang spirit is so marked among these Nazis; and it explains, too, why there has always seemed something unhealthy, abnormal, perverted, crawlingly corrupt, about them and all their activities.

And any country that allows itself to be dominated by the Nazis will not only have the German Gestapo crawling everywhere, but will also find itself in the power of all its own most unpleasant types—the very people who, for years, have been rotten with unsatisfied vanity, gnawing envy, and haunted by dreams of cruel power. Let the Nazis in, and you will find that the laziest loud-mouth in the workshop has suddenly been given power to kick you up and down the street, and that if you try to make any appeal, you have to do it to the one man in the district whose every word and look you'd always distrusted.

And as I thought these things going home the other night, there came the recollection of a tiny paragraph I'd seen in the papers that morning. It said that a German woman—like so many thousands of others, the hopelessly mentally distressed victim of Nazi persecution—had been found drowned in the Thames, and had left the following message: "I have had much kindness in England, but I decided to leave this world. May England be victorious." And I asked myself earnestly if really there was anything more to be said at this supreme hour than that.

If the kindness of England, of Britain, of the wide Empire forever reaching out towards new expressions of Freedom, is overshadowed by that vast dark face, then we all might as well decide to leave this world, for it will not be a world worth living in. But, she cried: "May England be victorious." And we can only reply to that poor tormented spirit: "England *will* be victorious."

Sunday, 30th June, 1940

THE other day in that bit of Old London that Shakespeare and Dickens knew—the Borough—a man was fined fifteen shillings for being drunk and disorderly. It seems that after the air-raid warning went, this man insisted upon standing in the middle of the street and loudly singing "Rule Britannia!"

Now, of course, it simply won't do to refuse to take cover during an air-raid or to be drunk and disorderly. I make no excuses for our friend from the Borough. Yet, between ourselves, I can't help feeling that when he stood there and sang Rule Britannia, he had the right idea. And I also can't help feeling that a great many other people here who will never be fined for being drunk and disorderly, or sing in the streets, have the wrong idea of how to treat this war. Sometimes I feel that you and I —all of us ordinary people—are on one side of a high fence, and on the other side of this fence under a buzzing cloud of secretaries, are the official and important personages: the pundits, and mandarins of the Fifth Button! and now and then a head appears above the fence and tells us to carry our gas masks, look to our blackouts, do this and attend to that.

"Certainly," we cry. "And how is the war?" "Sh, sh,

sh, sh!——" says the official voice, and the head, wearing a frown, disappears.

Is this too fanciful? Then I'll speak plainer. I think there is still too much pretence in some official quarters, that what we are living through now is really a kind of ordinary life, only much drearier; and the idea in such quarters is to try and make it drearier still.

Now if I'd my way I'd reverse this. I'd tell people to forget their old ordinary life because ultimately, anyhow, we'll either have a better life than that, or bust; and I'd order them about a bit—stop doing that, come and do this. If we're in a fortress, then let's behave like members of a garrison and not like members of a club during spring-cleaning.

But then, having done that, having ordered people about and bounced them out of their ordinary life, I'd stop making everything dreary and try and create as much fun, colour, romance as possible. I'd have bands playing everywhere, and flags flying, and as much swagger and glamour as the moment will stand.

There's nothing trivial and light-minded about this. We want hard work, but not hard looks; we need long endurance, but not long faces. It isn't woolly, pussy-footed officialdom that will win this war, but the courage, endurance and rising spirits of the British people. And we're still, as we always have been, at heart an imaginative and romantic people. And now that is the touch we need.

On the second day of this war, I wrote an article called "Two Ton Annie." I'd been watching some invalids from mainland hospitals being evacuated to the Isle of

Wight, and among these invalids was a very large, elderly woman, who was sitting upright on her stretcher and being carried by six staggering, sweating, grinning bearers, who called her "Two Ton Annie". She exchanged cheerful, insulting remarks with everybody. She was a roaring and indomitable old lioness, and wherever she was carried there was a cheerful tumult; and as she roared out repartee she saluted the grinning crowd like a raffish old empress. Yes; she was old, fat, helplessly lame and was being taken away from her familiar surroundings, a sick woman, far from home. But she gave no sign of any inward distress, but was her grand, uproarious self.

She did all our hearts good that day, and I said then that although Britannia can put up a good fight, Two Ton Annie and all her kind can put up a better one. I said that if it comes to a struggle between them and worried, semi-neurotic, police-ridden populations for ever raising their hands in solemnly idiotic salutes, standing to attention while the radio screams blasphemous nonsense at them, these people will emerge victorious because their sort of life breeds kindness, humour and courage, and the other sort of life doesn't.

Kindness, humour and courage are mightily sustaining qualities. They prevent that breakdown inside upon which our enemies with their screaming bogy-machines always depend.

Well, that was Two Ton Annie, who gave me such a heartening glimpse of our folk at the very beginning of the war. Since then, I'll confess, I've had glimpses that were much less heartening—in fact were even depressing.

For weeks, perhaps months, somehow Two Ton Annie and her uproarious stretcher-bearers and admirers disappeared, and instead I encountered another set of figures who might be described as Complacent Clarence, Hush-Hush Harold, and Dubious Departmental Desmond! These gentlemen have their places in our wartime scheme of things: this is not an attack upon them and their like; but often I couldn't help feeling, as a man who'd tried for years to understand our national character, that there was a real danger of these pundits and mandarins creating a rather thick, woolly, dreary atmosphere in which that national character of ours couldn't flourish and express itself properly.

The war, to which we have brought a unity of feeling never known before in our island history, was somehow not quite our war. Nobody told us right out to mind our own business, but often something of the sort was implied. There were too many snubs and cold-shoulders about. That was before the Blitzkrieg began. Since then, and especially since the danger crept nearer and the screaming threats grew louder and louder, I feel that that fog and its whispering figures have almost vanished, and that at any moment now I may encounter again my old friend Two Ton Annie.

Through the fading mists there emerge the simple, kindly, humorous brave faces of the ordinary British folk —a good people, deeply religious at heart, not only when they're kneeling in our little grey country churches but also when they're toiling at their machines or sweating under loads in the threatened dockyards.

Yes, a good people, who deep in their hearts only wish

to do what they feel is God's will. On them, on us, on all of you listening to me now, there rests the responsibility of manning this last great defence of our liberal civilisation. Already the future historians are fastening their gaze upon us, seeing us all in that clear and searching light of the great moments of history. That light may discover innumerable past follies and weaknesses of policy and national endeavour, but here and now, as the spirit of the people rises to meet the challenge, I believe that it will find no flaw in the sense, courage and endurance of those people.

All that they ask, all that we ask, is for more and more commands to the garrison; and then—well—let the bands play and the flags fly, and the people sing in the streets.

As Chesterton once sang:

> Rise up and bid the trumpets blow
> When it is gallant to be gay;
> Tell the wide world it shall not know
> Our face until we turn at bay.

Now I'll tell you the two most heartening and inspiring things I've seen this week.

The first was a duck; and the second was a dig in the ribs!

Now, in order to appreciate the duck you have to have some idea of the whole setting of the scene. It was rather late the other night, and we were coming home to Highgate Village by way of High-street, Hampstead, and the Spaniards-road, which run, you might say, on the roof of London. We had to pass the Whitestone Pond. Now I like the Whitestone Pond. On fine afternoons, boys sail their toy boats on it, and when there's a wind blowing across the Heath the toy boats have to battle with enormous waves—about three inches high. At night, this pond is like a little hand-mirror that the vast, sprawling, yawning London still holds negligently; and you see the stars glimmering in it. Well, the other night was one of those mysterious nights we've had lately when there seems to be a pale light coming from nowhere, and the sky has a pure washed look. The dim lights of a few cars could be seen in the dusk round the pond, and some people, late as it was, were standing and staring.

We stopped, and heard a solicitous quacking and a

great deal of faint squeaking. Then we saw on the pond, like a tiny feathered flotilla, a duck accompanied by her minute ducklings, just squeaking specks of yellow fluff. We joined the fascinated spectators; we forgot the war, the imminence of invasion, the doubts about the French Fleet, the melancholy antics of the Bordeaux Government.

Our eyes, and ears, and our imagination were caught and held by those triumphant little parcels of life. This duck hadn't hatched her brood here; she'd hatched them in some hidden corner—nobody knows where—and had then conveyed them—and nobody knows how—to swim happily in the dusk on this summit of the city. She hadn't asked anybody's advice or permission; she hadn't told herself it was too late or too difficult; nobody had told her to "Go to it" and that "it all depended on her". She had gone to it, a triumphant little servant of that life, mysterious, fruitful, beautiful, which expresses itself as a man writes a poem—now in vast galaxies of flaming suns, now in a tiny brood of ducklings squeaking in the dusk.

And if we forgot the war for a moment, afterwards we returned to think of it with a new courage, as if by that pond we'd been given a sign. For reduced to its very simplest but profoundest terms, this is a war between despair and hope; for Nazism is really the most violent expression of the despair of the modern world. It's the black abyss at the end of a wrong road. It's a negation of the good life. It is at heart death-worship. But there flows through all nature a tide of being, a creative energy that at every moment challenges and contradicts this death-worship of despairing, crazy men. Even the mallard duck, bringing from nowhere its happy little cargo of life, salutes us in the growing darkness and tells us to stand up and fight and be of good courage.

The second of these two most heartening and inspiring things of the week was, as I said, a dig in the ribs! It wasn't a dig in my ribs; and then again, it wasn't so much the dig as the grin that went with it. But I'd better explain.

It happened on Thursday afternoon. I went to the House of Commons to hear the Prime Minister make his statement on the French Fleet. It was, as you all know by this time, a most exciting and heartening afternoon. The deepening undercurrent of excitement during the question time that preceded the statement the rapidly-filling benches and galleries of the House, the sombre opening and triumphant conclusion of the Premier's speech, the tumultuous reception of it by the whole standing, cheering House. But all this you have heard already.

What specially heartened and inspired me was a tiny thing that happened long before these fireworks were exploded. Mr. Churchill entered the House, not to make his statement but to answer one or two questions. He was greeted, as well he might be, with that peculiar "hear-hearing" that is described by parliamentary reporters as "cheers". His head was sunk into his broad shoulders, giving him that characteristic bull-dog look. His face was set, unsmiling, grave. He looked indeed what we knew him to be—a man called upon to take terrible decisions, to remove the sword from the hand of a friend who is beginning to forget the solemn oaths with which that sword had been unsheathed.

Now, next to the place on the Front Bench towards which Mr. Churchill was now slowly making his way was Mr. Ernest Bevin, who had been answering questions on the paper—and answering them with promptness and vigour: a powerful, thick-set, determined figure of a man, a fine lump of that England which we all love; one of those men who stand up among the cowardices and treacheries and corruption of this recent world like an oak tree in a swamp. So Mr. Churchill, representing you might say the other half of the English people and English history, moved slowly to his place next to the massive, yeoman figure of Mr. Bevin; and for a second or so, still meditating deeply on what he had to say, he kept the withdrawn, unsmiling look with which he had entered.

But then, coming out of his reverie and recognising who was beside him, Mr. Churchill gave his colleague a sharp little punch of greeting—a little dig in the ribs; and as he did this there flashed across his face a sudden boyish, mischievous, devil-may-care grin. And I said to myself "these are the men for me". I said to myself as if I'd suddenly turned back twenty-five years and was a corporal of infantry again: "That's the stuff to give 'em!"

You know, I'm always being asked by somebody or other to talk to you about these slogans that are produced by experts, but somehow I never quite take to them; but if they were anything like as good as "that's the stuff to give 'em!" I'd talk about them until the microphone began to steam. And now after years I found myself crying exultantly again: "That's the stuff to give 'em!" because Mr. Churchill, a man in his sixties who has driven himself as hard as he could go ever since Omdurman, who has held high office for more than thirty years, and upon whose shoulders now rests perhaps the fate of Europe for centuries, could in this grave hour to which he had done full justice both in his private decision and his public utterances, let slip that wonderful, lightning grin which was like a miraculous glimpse of the inner man who, like so many formidable men, is still a boy at heart, still full of devilment. And I said to myself that this is the kind of man the English, and the Scots, and the Welsh, and for that matter the Irish, want at this challenging hour, and no weary gentlemanly muddling and mumbling of platitudes.

When I saw that grin and that dig in the ribs, I said: "These are the men for us, but let them make haste, raise their voices and command the expectant people, who can, out of their kindness, humour and courage, yet defeat these cunning, ruthless but crack-brained and small-hearted Nazis.

Let them cry at once, with Shakespeare, to the waiting people:

"For there is none of you so mean and base
    That hath not noble lustre in your eyes.
        I see you stand like greyhounds in the slips,
        Straining upon the start. The game's afoot:
        Follow your spirit; and, upon this charge
    Cry: 'God for Harry, England and Saint George'. "

Sunday, 14th July, 1940

THE other day I made the strangest journey I ever remember making in this country: I went to Margate. But of course it wasn't like any possible kind of visit to Margate that we could have imagined before this war; it was like some fantastic dream of a day trip to Margate. A dozen times during the day I told myself that in a minute I'd wake up from all this, and find myself back in the comfortable routine of a year ago. I didn't pinch myself—I believe people only do that in rather carelessly written novels—but I think several times I sort of mentally pinched myself, to discover if I were awake.

The start wasn't unusual except that we all had a lot of passes and permits, and we took tin hats along with us too; so that if a lot of stuff came down we'd have our portable little air-raid shelters. Some people despise tin hats—but not me. I remember them first arriving in the trenches—and very glad we were to see them, too.

Well, we set off for Margate—and for some time it was all quite ordinary, but after that it soon began to seem rather peculiar. Along the road there were things that weren't quite what they first appeared to be—if you see what I mean; the Bren guns seemed to be getting mixed up with the agricultural life of north Kent. The most flourishing crop seemed to be barbed wire. Soldiers would pop up from nowhere and then vanish again—unless they wanted to see our permits. Some extra large greenish cattle, quietly pasturing underneath the elms, might possibly have been tanks. It was a rum sort of farming round there!—and then as we came nearer the East Coast, the place seemed emptier and emptier. There were signs and portents. A field would have a hole in it, made at the expense of considerable time, trouble, and outlay of capital, by the German Air Force. An empty bungalow, minus its front door and dining-room, stared at us in mute reproach. An R.A.F. lorry went past, taking with it the remains of a Heinkel bomber.

We were almost on the front at Margate before I'd realised that we were anywhere near the town—although *I* was holding the map! I must say that if any invaders are going anywhere in particular, and not just wandering about, they're in for a very puzzling time; and I can't help feeling that while they're trying to make out where they are, whole packets of trouble will come their way.

But there we were at last—on the front at Margate. The sun, with a fine irony, came bounding out. The sea, which has its own sense of humour, winked and sparkled at us. We began to walk along the front. Everything was there: bathing pools, bandstands, gardens blazing with flowers, lido, theatres, and the like; and miles of firm golden sands all spread out beneath the July sun. But no people!—not a soul. Of all those hundreds of thousands of holiday-makers, of entertainers and hawkers and boatmen—not one. And no sound—not the very ghost of an echo of all that cheerful hullabaloo—

children shouting and laughing, bands playing, concert parties singing, men selling ice-cream, whelks and peppermint rock, which I'd remembered hearing along this shore. No, not even an echo. Silence. It was as if an evil magician had whisked everybody away. There were the rows and rows of boarding-houses, the "Sea Views" and "Bryn Mawrs" and "Craig-y-dons" and "Sans Soucis" and the rest, which ought to have been bursting with life, with red faces, piano and gramophone music, and the smell of roast beef and Yorkshire pudding, but all empty, shuttered, forlorn. A most melancholy boarding-house at the end of a row caught my eye—and that one was called "Kismet". Kismet, indeed!

In search of a drink and a sandwich, we wandered round, and sometimes through, large empty hotels. The few signs of life only made the whole place seem more unreal and spectral. Once an ancient taxi came gliding along the promenade, and we agreed that if we'd hailed it, making a shout in that silence, it would have dissolved at once into thin air. An elderly postman on a bicycle may have been real or yet another apparition.

At last we found a café open, somewhere at the back of the town, and had no sooner had our roast mutton and green peas set in front of us, than the sirens began screaming. But after all this strange ghostliness, an air-raid warning didn't seem to matter much; and we finished our mutton and had some pancakes. The "All Clear" found us in a small bar about two miles away, where one of the patrons—a fat man in his shirt-sleeves—observed placidly: "Well, I fancy there ought to be another one just about six." After noting this evidence of

the "terrible panic" among the remaining inhabitants of
the south-east coast of Britain, we returned to con-
template, still under its strange spell, this bright ghost of a
Margate. I remembered so vividly a day I'd spent here
ten years ago, when the whole coast was crammed and
noisy with folk and it was all a jolly, sweaty
pandemonium. Had that been a dream?—or was this
strange silent afternoon a dream? It seemed impossible
that they should both be real. Yet here we were, alone,
hearing our own footfalls on the lifeless promenade. The
evil magician had muttered the enchanted phrase—and a
wind had come from Hell and blown away all the
trippers and paddlers and pierrots and hawkers—all that
perspiring, bustling, rowdy, riotous holiday-making.

And as I stood there, half bemused in the blazing
ironic sunshine, I asked myself what I would do if
another and better magician should arrive and tell me
that he had only to wave *his* wand to send time hurtling
back, so that once again these sands would be thick with
honest folk, the boarding-houses bursting again with
buckets and spades and the smell of cabbage; the bandstands and stages as lively as ever. Would I agree?
Would I say?: "Yes, let time go back. Let this melancholy
silent afternoon be only a dream of an impossible
Margate. Say the word, and let Margate—and West-
gate, and Herne Bay and Broadstairs and Ramsgate and
a hundred other resorts—be as they were a year ago."

And I said No, I want no such miracle. Let this be
real, so far as all this muddled groping of ours with the
deep purposes of life can be considered real—and let time
tick on. But if you would help us, then, if you are a great

and wise magician, move our minds and hearts towards
steadfast courage and faith and hope, because we're
ready to accept all this: the silent town that once was
gay; vanished crowds now toiling far from these vacant
sands; this hour of trial and testing—if we know that we
can march forward—not merely to recover what has
been lost, but to something better than we've ever known
before.

That's what I would have said to that magician. And
now I say to all of you who are listening, for in your
common will there is an even mightier magician: This
Margate I saw was saddening and hateful; but its new
silence and desolation should be thought of as a bridge
leading us to a better Margate in a better England, in a
nobler world. We're not fighting to restore the past; it
was the past that brought us to this heavy hour; but we
are fighting to rid ourselves and the world of the evil
encumbrance of these Nazis so that we can plan and
create a noble future for all our species.

"I think that in the coming time the hearts and hopes oɪ
   men
The mountain tops of life shall climb, the gods return
   again.
I strive to blow the magic horn; it feebly murmureth,
Arise on some enchanted morn, fight with God's own
   breath,
And sound the horn I cannot blow, and by the secret
   name
Each exile of the heart will know, kindle the magic
   flame."

I HADN'T been in his room more than two minutes when this official and I were looking at each other as a cat looks at a dog. We just weren't getting on at all. I ought to have known we wouldn't get on. And we hadn't been together five minutes, this official and I, before I knew that he knew what I thought about him, and he knew that I knew what he was thinking about me. He saw me as an impatient, slapdash, dangerous sort of fellow, wanting everything done all at once, bringing out all manner of half-digested notions and bragging, swaggering, insufferably pleased with myself, rather a bounder and an outsider, really. And I saw him as a coldly conceited, ungenerous, sterile kind of chap, never throwing himself wholeheartedly into anything, always wondering how he was going to come out of it, and just as he'd call me a bounder I'd call him "a stuffed shirt".

Well, there we were, not getting on at all and taking a greater and greater dislike to each other. But his manners, being better trained than mine, hadn't worn quite so thin. He made those little movements that politely suggest to a caller that it's time to go. He said: "We might be able to form a small sub-committee; then, perhaps you'd like to send in some kind of report, just a short memo, embodying . . ." And I said: "No, I don't think so. Good morning," and went. And he said to himself: "Well, thank goodness I've got rid of that fellow, barging in here as if he owned the place. He can't begin to understand our difficulties, relations with the Treasury and so on"; and I said to myself: "Stuffed shirts and Mandarins, oh dear, oh dear, oh dear, oh dear, oh dear." Two entirely different and opposed types of mind and temperament, you see, the warmly imaginative against the coldly rational, the slapdash against the punctilious, the impatient against the cautious, the creative against the administrative. Clearly we must have both types of mind working now at full pressure and it's absolutely essential that each should have its own sphere of activity. It's in the relation of eager, imaginative, creative minds and cool, punctilious, administrative minds that we've tended to go wrong. That abortive interview I've just described is probably typical of what happens.

Now, there are two ways of looking at this war. The first way, which, on the whole, we are officially encouraged to adopt, is to see this war as a terrible interruption. As soon as we can decently do it, we must return to what is called peace, so let's make all the munitions we can, and be ready to do some hard fighting, and then we can have done with Hitler and his Nazis and go back to where we started from, the day before war was declared. Now this, to my mind, is all wrong. It's wrong because it simply isn't true. A year ago, though we hadn't actually declared war, there wasn't real peace, or the year before, or the year before that. If you go back to the sort of world that produces Hitlers and Mussolinis, then no sooner have you got rid of one lot of Hitlers and Mussolinis than another lot will pop up somewhere, and there'll be more wars.

This brings us to the second, and more truthful, way of looking at this war. That is, to regard this war as one chapter in a tremendous history, the history of a changing world, the breakdown of one vast system and the building up of another and better one. In this view of things Hitler and Mussolini have been thrown up by this breakdown of a world system. It's as if an earthquake cracked the walls and floors of a house and strange nuisances of things, Nazists and Fascists, came running out of the woodwork. We have to get rid of these intolerable nuisances but not so that we can go *back* to anything. There's nothing that really worked that we can go back to. But so that we can go forward, without all the shouting and stamping and bullying and murder, and really plan and build up a nobler world in which ordinary, decent folk can not only find justice and security but also beauty and delight. And this isn't a "pipe dream" because many of our difficulties have arrived not because man's capacity is feebler than it used to be, but just because it's actually so much greater. The modern man, thanks to his inventiveness, has suddenly been given a hundred arms and seven-league boots. But we can't go forward and build up this new world order, and this is our real war aim, unless we begin to think differently, and my own personal view, for what it's worth, is that we must stop thinking in terms of property and power and begin thinking in terms of community and creation.

Now, I'll explain just what I mean. First, take the change from power to creation. Now, power—whether on a large or small scale—really boils down to the ignoble pleasure of bossing and ordering other people about because you have the whip-hand of them. All these Nazi and Fascist leaders are power worshippers, they're almost drunk on it. I suspect it's simply a bad substitute for the joy of creation, which everybody understands, whether you're creating a vast educational system or a magnificent work of art, or bringing into existence a vegetable garden or a thundering good dinner. People are never so innocently happy as when they're creating something. So, we want a world that offers people not the dubious pleasures of power, but the maximum opportunities for creation. And even already, in the middle of this war, I can see that world shaping itself.

And now we'll take the change from property to community. Property is that old-fashioned way of thinking of a country as a thing, and a collection of things on that thing, all owned by certain people and constituting property; instead of thinking of a country as the home of a living society, and considering the welfare of that society, the community itself, as the first test. And I'll give you an instance of how this change should be working. Near where I live is a house with a large garden, that's not being used at all because the owner of it has gone to America. Now, according to the property view, this is all right, and we, who haven't gone to

America, must fight to protect this absentee owner's
property. But on the community view, this is all wrong.
There are hundreds of working men not far from here
who urgently need ground for allotments so that they can
produce a bit more food. Also, we may soon need more
houses for billeting. Therefore, I say, that house and
garden ought to be used whether the owner, who's gone
to America, likes it or not. That's merely one instance,
and you can easily find dozens of others.

Now, the war, because it demands a huge collective
effort, is compelling us to change not only our ordinary,
social and economic habits, but also our habits of
thought. We're actually changing over from the
property view to the sense of community, which simply
means that we realise we're all in the same boat. But,
and this is the point, that boat can serve not only as our
defence against Nazi aggression, but as an ark in which
we can all finally land in a better world. And when I
say We, I don't mean only the British and their allied
peoples, but all people everywhere, including all the
Germans who haven't sold themselves body and soul to
the evil Nazi idea. I tell you, there is stirring in us now, a
desire which could soon become a controlled but
passionate determination to remodel and recreate this
life of ours, to make it the glorious beginning of a new
world order, so that we might soon be so fully and
happily engrossed in our great task that if Hitler and his
gang suddenly disappeared we'd hardly notice that
they'd gone. We're even now the hope of free men
everywhere but soon we could be the hope and lovely
dawn of the whole wide world.

Sunday, 28th July, 1940

NOT long ago I had the privilege of attending a little family party. This party was given to celebrate the safe return of the youngest member of his family, who's a Pilot Officer in the Royal Air Force. He and his crew—that implies a big bombing plane—had been missing for many hours; they'd spent these hours in a rubber dinghy on the North Sea, but now, with nothing worse than a bruised hand and arm, he was on leave, with his pretty young wife in attendance at this party.

He hadn't changed very much, really: it was I who stared at him with new eyes, as if I were meeting a figure from some epic—a cheerful young giant out of a saga. Before the war I used to spend an occasional Sunday playing lawn tennis with his family, and now and again he would turn up, in a battered little sports car, with this same pretty girl in attendance—a tall, casual but friendly lad, who played an enthusiastic but slapdash game of tennis with one of those terrific first services that nearly always go miles out, but when they do hit the court are winners.

I knew—for I'd heard him mention it casually—that he piloted heavy bombers—but to what kind of life he went roaring back in his little car, I'd no idea—and, to

be truthful, I wasn't interested. I'd never even seen him
in uniform: I saw him as a nice, long-legged, untidy lad,
putting in a few years in the Air Force until he thought of
something more serious to do. And then the other day
we met again—and talked; though that wasn't too easy
at first because he was shy and modest and absurdly
respectful to this middle-aged civilian.

To realise properly and appreciate what he'd done
and where he'd been, since the beginning of last September you have to bring out your map of Europe, then let
your eye range from the Arctic Circle to the Gulf of
Genoa. Norway, Denmark, Germany, Holland, Belgium,
France, Italy—he'd flown over them all, and had had to
find in them certain points far too small to be marked on
any maps that you and I possess—an aerodrome, a
railway station, one particular factory, a certain cross-
roads. And in the R.A.F. you have to find what you've
been sent out to find—you have your target, and there is
no nonsense about unloading your bombs merely in its
vicinity.

Night after night—at first carrying pamphlets, then,
in the dread cold of winter, making reconnaissance
flights, and ever since, carrying bombs—he's gone
roaring out of his aerodrome in England, over the North
Sea, over strange darkened lands far to the North, far to
the East, far to the South, to come circling down where
coloured searchlights went wheeling and there would be
a golden hail of tracer bullets, and the earth below
belched and spat its anti-aircraft fire, and there was the
thresh and the shudder of exploding bombs. And then
he'd turn, and lift the great machine towards home, and

see the pale-washed light of dawn spread over the floor of cloud or far below over the cold tumbling seas, and then see at last the familiar pattern of fields, and wonder if there were sausages or bacon for breakfast in the mess. And not all who set out would always come back— "From these operations," the easy glib phrase runs, "two of our aircraft are missing." Empty chairs in the mess—letters in the rack which will never be claimed— shadows of eyes and dying echoes of voices—they pass and smile, the children of the sword.

So that's his life; and though I've given you not even a glimpse of what is exacting and responsible in it, the actual piloting of these great vessels of the air across thousand of miles—the intricate co-operation both on land and in the air—the response to all those severe demands made by our Royal Air Force upon all its personnel. But let us remember now that pretty young wife. She lodges as close as regulations permit to the aerodrome, so that her husband can dash out now and again at lunchtime and see her. In the evenings she hears the Squadron take the air for its new adventure, knowing no more than you and I would know where they're going; but she counts the planes as they go roaring up. Then, hours and hours afterwards, some- where around dawn, after a series of uneasy broken naps, she hears the faint familiar drone of the returning bombers; sits up, and above the loud beating of her heart, counts the planes that have come safely home. One—two—three—and so on, until there's silence again; and if the total is the same as it was when she counted them going up, then it's all right—it must be all right, and at last she can go to sleep. But if it isn't the same, then there's no more chance of sleep for her. And that's her life these days.

A year ago these were just a pair of light-hearted youngsters, dashing about in their battered little car, and even now, on leave, as I met them, they're a light-hearted pair still. Nevertheless, that's their life, and it's passed in our service. And what I want to know now is this: it's all right feeling a lump in the throat, and saying "God bless you", but what are we really going to do about it?

I will tell you what we did for such young men and their young wives at the end of the last war. We did nothing—except let them take their chance in a world in which every gangster and trickster and stupid insensitive fool or rogue was let loose to do his damnedest. After the cheering and the flag-waving were over, and all the medals were given out, somehow the young heroes disappeared, but after a year or two there were a lot of shabby, young-oldish men about who didn't seem to have been lucky in the scramble for easy jobs and quick profits, and so tried to sell us second-hand cars or office supplies we didn't want, or even trailed round the suburbs asking to be allowed to demonstrate the latest vacuum cleaner.

No doubt it's going to be all different this time, but some of us can't help discovering, to our dismay, that the same sort of minds are still about. Among bundles of very friendly letters just lately I've been getting some very fierce and angry ones telling me to get off the air before the Government "puts you where you belong"— the real Fascist touch. Well, obviously, it wouldn't matter much if I were taken off the air, but it would matter a great deal, even to these Blimps, if these young men of the R.A.F. were taken off the air; and so I repeat my question—in return for their skill, devotion, endurance and self-sacrifice, what are we civilians prepared to do? And surely the answer is that the least we can do is to give our minds honestly, sincerely and without immediate self-interest, to the task of preparing a world really fit for them and their kind—to arrange for them a final "happy landing".

Don't insult them by thinking they don't care what sort of a world they're fighting for. All the evidence contradicts that. And here's a bit of it in a letter that reached me a day or two ago. It runs as follows:

"My son was formerly a salesman; he resigned in order to join the Air Force. On a recent visit home he said: 'I shall never go back to the old business life—that life of what I call the survival of the slickest; I now know a better way. Our lads in the R.A.F. would, and do, willingly give their lives for each other; the whole outlook of the force is one of 'give', not one of 'get'. If to-morrow the war ended and I returned to business, I would need to sneak, cheat and pry in order to get hold of orders which otherwise would have gone to one of my R.A.F. friends if one of them returned to commercial life with a competing firm. Instead of co-operating as we do in war, we would each use all the craft we possessed with which to confound each other. I will never do it."

His father ends by saying: "You, sir, will be able to adorn this tale—it's a true one—I hope you will." But I don't think it needs any adorning.

Sunday, 4th August, 1940

TWENTY-SIX years ago to-day, the 4th August, Great Britain declared war on Germany which had already moved to violate the neutrality of Belgium. Oddly enough, I can remember nothing about this day, which was a Tuesday, although I have a sharp recollection of the evening before, that of Bank Holiday Monday. That part of Bradford where I lived then, had its annual fair at that season—it was called Manningham Tide. And I remember going to this fair with a friend, a young artist, and explaining the international situation to him on our way home. It was the last time I ever knew the glitter and jangle of Manningham Tide—it vanished, and with it vanished a whole world. I remember, too, how hot it was during those first days of August 1914. My feet used to swell and ache in my stiff Brogue shoes—it never seems to be as hot as that now.

A queer chap I knew had insisted, that summer, on telling my fortune, by cards, and had told me, earnestly, that I was about to change my whole way of living; that often I would be in great danger, that my life would never be the same again after all this strange, desperate journey. And I didn't believe a word of it. But it was all true. On August 4th war was declared, on the 5th Kitchener became Secretary of State for War, and on the 7th he appealed for the first hundred thousand men.

Already, as I went whirling round the switchbacks to the tune of "Hitchy Koo" the three blind Fates were cutting the threads of a million destinies. Half my generation was doomed, and at the fair I was seeing for the last time many a face I had known since I was a child. Well, there it was, this change in my whole way of living, as the fortune-teller said, a change indeed, from one world to another.

Do you ever look back on your life, and see it as a road that wanders through wildly varying landscapes? I do. And now, as I look back, before August 1914 the road seems to be in a sunlit plain, coming out of the mists of early childhood. Then, for the next four or five years, the road goes through black and terrible mountains, and is sometimes almost obliterated by avalanches. It comes out into 1919 and enters a confused landscape, with swamps and dark forests and sudden pleasant uplands. These were the years of the false peace, of the defeat of good will. There was plenty of good will about in those nineteen-twenties—it's a sad mistake to think there wasn't—but somehow it couldn't secure adequate representation. It let the old hands, the experts, the smooth gentry who assure you that your inexperience tends to make you gravely underestimate the difficulties of the situation, speak for it, and they sold it out.

Then came the 'Thirties, and that road descended into a stony wilderness of world depression and despair; and very soon in that desert, fantastically shaped rocks and cruel jagged ridges began to show themselves, and soon there were more and more of them, closer and closer to the road; until at last it climbed and narrowed to a track between iron-edged boulders and sometimes clinging to the edge of precipices.

These were the years when it was evident that the war had started all over again, assuming new and even more sinister forms, when we were appalled by the violence and cruelty hidden in the modern man's depths of despair. Great lie machines were installed in Central Europe, and far below them, in bloodstained basements, were official torture chambers.

We were now to be shown how men can behave when they have lost all hope of the Kingdom of Heaven, how when you have robbed men of all belief in this or any other world, the first madman who arrives can capture them with his fantasies. And so the disguised war of the 'Thirties became the open war of 1940.

This war is quite unlike the one that broke out twenty-six years ago. Have you ever noticed how all the attempts—and there have been many—to see this war in terms of the last, have failed? You just can't give this war a "Tipperary", "Keep the Home Fires Burning" flavour. It won't have it. The queer thing is that these attempts, which have been deliberate and often well organised, are frustrated by masses of people who could give no explanation of why they shrug their shoulders and turn away. I suspect that the wisest historian resides somewhere in the collective unconscious minds of whole populations. You can't deceive that mysterious fellow. He knows that this conflict is not a repetition of the last war. I think all our people here know it, too, in their hearts, and this explains why they respond so eagerly to really new appeals to their loyalty, and don't respond to the old routine stuff, of which they've been given far too much. They notice, for example, that the old strictly nationalistic divisions don't quite fit. There are millions of Germans who are praying that Hitler will lose. There may be some Britons, of a certain psychological type, persons hungry for power at all costs, who would like Hitler to win.

The history of France in these two wars offers the most vivid and significant illustration of the profound difference between these wars. And I feel that the popular mind, though perhaps for the most part rather obscurely, understands this difference much better than many of our official minds. This isn't 1914. It isn't simply a question of Germans fighting for Germany and Britons for Britain. And—Communists here and abroad, please note—it certainly isn't a question of who shall collect the dividends of some African trading company. You couldn't get people to fight five minutes on such an issue.

Reduced to its simplest, but profoundest, terms, this is a war between despair and hope. Nazism, beneath its show of efficiency and organisation, its triumphant nationalism at home and its revolutionary propaganda talk abroad, has a basis of complete and utter despair, its one belief being that man is a contemptible creature, incapable of finding any truth anywhere, to be ruled by alternate doses of crude flattery and cruel punishment, a fool, a liar, a coward, a perpetual cheat. It is significant that not one Nazi leader has ever been associated with any great movement to uphold and strengthen the dignity and nobility of mankind. They came, like their vile creed, from an underworld of despair and hate. To oppose these men and their evil doctrine we must not only summon our armed forces, wave our flags and sing our national anthems, but we must go deeper and, by an almost mystical act of will, hold to our faith and our hope. We have to fight this great battle not only with guns in daylight, but alone in the night, communing with our souls, strengthening our faith that in common men everywhere there is a spring of innocent aspiration and good will that shall not be sealed. This is the real test. If we have men on our side who don't share this faith and hope, then let them leave us and join the armies of despair. But whoever shares this faith and hope, no matter to what race they belong or what language they speak, let them be welcomed as allies. And this test remains for all policies from now on. If such policies, and all the actions resulting from them, enlarge and strengthen this faith, this great hope, then they will help us to victory, the only victory worth having, the final conquest of despair. Any sly, nasty, vindictive, utterly cynical policies and actions belong not to our side but to the other despairing mind with which we are at war.

And so much truth, at least, we have discovered on the long, hard road from August the Fourth 1914 to August the Fourth, 1940.

Sunday, 11th August, 1940

THE other day I saw two thousand people push aside
what remained of the meat pies and fried plaice and chips
they'd had for lunch, lift their eyes and ears towards an
orchestra consisting of four young women in green silk,
and then, all two thousand of them, roar out: "Oh
Johnny, Oh Johnny, How You Can Love". And having
paid this tribute to Johnny and applauded the four
young women in green silk, these two thousand people,
who were mostly young and feminine, and very natty in
their coloured overalls, returned—much heartened—to
another five or six hours' work at their machines.

Obviously, this genial conspiracy between the Ministry
of Labour and Ensa to provide entertainment during the
meal hours, at midday for the day shifts, at midnight for
the night shifts, for workers in the war factories, was a
roaring success.

I left that factory, which was a rather neat, ladylike
affair, for another in the neighbourhood, which was
grimmer and more masculine. Here I went through long
sheds shuddering with the din of drills and hammers.
The place vibrated with power. Partly to show off, and
partly to frighten me and keep me in my place, they took
me to a high, enclosed room, turned out the lights and

said they would give me a glimpse of the giant they'd turned tame to work for them. There was a sinister hum, there was an even more sinister violet glow, an unearthly demon light, and then a terrifying crack and flash of seven hundred and fifty thousand volts.

In another place you peeped through tiny windows into what looked like ovens, and in there—dressed to look like divers or perhaps creatures from Mars—were men shot-blasting. In other places, they were peering through masks at strange, brilliant lights, and looked like wizards, but were actually electric welders. Everywhere else, shed after shed, quivering belts and clanging machines. If you work in there you have to attend to these machines, which stand no nonsense from you, from ten to eleven hours a day.

No wonder then that in the canteen, once the last chip had been eaten and cigarettes and pipes were alight, that small, select Concert Party "The Night Howls" was rapturously received. Jokes that had seen service in pantomime with many a Widow Twankey and Baron Hardup were hailed with as much delight as if they had been newly minted and shining with wit. That packed canteen was a comedian's paradise, and it must have done the entertainers themselves, who would return there at one in the morning, all the good in the world to watch the lines smooth out in the faces before them and see tired eyes brighten with laughter. I know it did me good, and I was glad to learn from Mr. Basil Dean how very soon there would be no less than a hundred and twenty concert parties entertaining these war workers in every corner of the country.

I've always had a soft spot for Mr. Dean, and his Ensa organisation, because I remember how, in a dreary, remote camp, in the melancholy winter of 1917, the companies he sent to our Garrison Theatre coloured and brightened my evenings. And it was a fine human impulse of the Minister of Labour, to bring at least an hour or two's cheerful entertainment to these war workers, who, for these past few months, have been asked to increase their output to the very maximum. There will, of course, be persons listening now who will disapprove of all this. There are people who disapprove of everything, people who at heart wish we were all dead and buried. But I must tell them at once that, unless they are also putting in ten or eleven hours a day among the war machinery, I haven't much interest in their criticism. Comfortable persons who feel that munition workers are being overpaid and coddled, should accept the Government offer of training and try for a job in the factories themselves. But I warn them that, after a few spells of work among those belts and drills and hammers, they may find themselves packing in for their fried plaice and chips with the rest, and then joining in with enthusiasm in "Roll Out The Barrel". I'll admit that as a fortunate outsider, who hasn't to spend ten hours a day in a clanging factory and is shockingly overpraised for slinging a few artful phrases together, I don't particularly want to share my lunch-hour with young women in green silk playing piano-accordions, or find it necessary to smoke my after-lunch pipe at a couple of red-nosed, cross-talk comedians. But you've only to watch the people's faces, and hear their voices, to know that this idea of joining songs and high jinks to hard work is as sound as a bell. I'd like to see it extended.

If the Members of the Cabinet, who, after all, work still longer hours, should decide that a super Concert Party should visit Downing Street once or twice a week, I'd gladly make one of the party, as a super red-nosed comic, in which capacity—by the way—I rather fancy myself.

I say this idea of hard work and high jinks is so sound that it should be applied to much more than light entertainments in factory canteens. Just as the hard work can be handed out to more and more people, and we still hear them asking for it, so, too, the high jinks can be higher still. The people have said to authority here: "This is our war, command us; put great burdens on our shoulders." And authority, it should reply to the people: "If nothing is too great for you to bear, then nothing is too good for you to have. Whatever men have devised to uplift the heart, set fire to the imagination and release the spirit, that you shall have."

It's often been said, and too often by our own unrepresentative men, that we Islanders are a cold-hearted and unimaginative folk, and it's a thundering lie, for we have some of the most glorious witnesses to our warmth and heart, and height of imagination, from Shakespeare onwards, that the world can know. Always, when we've spoken or acted, as a people, and not when we've gone to sleep and allowed some Justice Shallow to represent us, that lift of the heart, that touch of the imagination, have been suddenly discovered in our speech and our affairs, giving our history a strange glow, the light that never was on sea or land.

And there are millions here who have had a glimpse—
but alas, no more than a glimpse, of a whole world of
beauty, have exclaimed in wonder and delight, and have
then seen it fade, and gone back, sick at heart, to their
dark workshops and mean streets. So I say—Let us, by
all means, have four young women in green silk playing
"Oh Johnny, Oh Johnny", but at the same time, let's
have the great symphony orchestras peeling out the
noblest music, night after night, not for a fortunate and
privileged few, but for all the people who long for such
music. Let's have comedians in the canteens, but at the
same time let's have productions of great plays in our
theatres, so that the people who work may also laugh,
and weep, and wonder. We must all have at least a
glimpse, while we labour or fight, of those glorious
worlds of the imagination from which come fitful gleams
to this sad, haunted earth. It may be possible yet, even
while we struggle and endure, and at last batter our way
through to victory, to achieve what's long been overdue
in this Island, and that is, not only to retain what's best
out of an old tradition, but to increase that heritage by
raising at last the quality of our life. No burden, it
seems, is too great for the people. Then there can't be
too rich and great a reward for the people.

Sunday, 25th August, 1940

YES, I had a very nice little holiday, thank you—and feel so much better that I'm going to take the risk of giving some of you a bit of advice. No, I'm not going to ask you to bring your children back from the country into the cities, though I do assure you that you oughtn't to bring them back. I'm not going to tell you that you really mustn't go crowding into areas that have just been bombed, though you mustn't because you get in the way of the people who are clearing up the mess. No, what I'm going to suggest is what seems to me the best way of mentally *coping* with this war. But before I do that, I'll tell you the *worst* way—how to drive yourself half barmy. You do this—God help you!—by chaining your mind to the procession of events, by reading in ten different newspapers and hearing in five news broadcasts about the same eleven Heinkels and seven Messerschmitts, by never stopping wondering in a dreary kind of fashion —you know—"I wonder what they'll try next," by opening your mind to nothing but idiotic rumours or lying enemy propaganda. Now the best way is the opposite of this. Don't be dragged along in that slow procession. Sometimes, take your mind clean away from the whole business, just break loose from it. But then,

come back to the War and instead of rumouring and
wondering, really *think* about it, cut through the surface,
and try to discover what's behind, pulling the strings, in
this vast lunatic puppet-show of armed men and
machines. In this way, instead of the War—as people
say—getting *you down*, you get *it* down, to take a good
look at it; and you begin to exercise, to be a part of, that
free, enquiring, searching mind that not all the bombs in
the world can destroy because it's unconquerable and
indestructible, it's—immortal.

Now, last Sunday, when I ought to have been talking
to you, I was recovering, with the help of a bright fire
and an unexpected treasure trove in the form of a flask of
whisky, from an adventure on a mountain in North
Wales, where we were staying. And very lovely it was
too in that remote valley, with the heather and ling in
bloom on the slopes, the moor birds crying above the
cold music of the waterfalls, and the little trout flickering
like shadows in the mountain streams. I am myself a
townsman but when I go into the country I prefer to be
remote—like Wordsworth—in high bare country—with

> The silence that is in the starry sky,
> The sleep that is among the lonely hills . . .

So here, last Sunday morning, two schoolgirl daughters
who wouldn't put any thick clothes on and just wouldn't
be told, and I, set out to climb a mountain. There was
only one decent way up and that was along the ridge,
and we swung up and along this ridge in great style and
before one o'clock had reached the summit. But now we
were lost in a cloud, couldn't see more than ten yards

clearly, and out of this thick mist came a bitter, drenching rain, cold as January. It was all right while we were sheltering behind a rock and eating and drinking, but it was all wrong when we began our descent. We were wet through, shivering, and too anxious to get back home. Especially the two girls, who just wouldn't listen to the feeble protests of their father, who pointed out that he ought to have a map and compass, but hadn't; that descending a mountain consisting mostly of steep, slaty, wet slopes, in a thick fog, is no joke at all, and that we ought to be very wary and though our teeth might be chattering, we ought to take it easy, go a few steps at a time, and not rush at it. But no, they said they remembered exactly which way we came up, though now we couldn't see anything, of course, and off they dashed, leaving me to follow them, bleating like an old sheep.

Well, I won't describe in detail how we completely lost ourselves in that chill, blank world, how we scrambled and slipped and peered over the edge of what looked like horrible precipices, and finally, after nearly breaking our necks a score of times, found ourselves past the worst slopes and descending into a valley. But then the mist lifted a little and we suddenly stopped congratulating ourselves, for we were near the edge of a lake, and we knew only too well that there was no lake in our valley, so that it was painfully obvious that we had come careering down the wrong side of the mountain and were miles and miles and miles from home.

Luckily we found a farmhouse near the lake, and inside it some very nice Welsh people—and the Welsh are very nice people—who've had the sense not to lose their time-old passion for sensible things like music and poetry—and so we were allowed to steam in front of a fire, given some hot tea, and at last driven over a bumpy little mountain road back home.

Now, if you say that isn't much of an adventure in these desperate days, I'd have to agree with you, though at the worst it's a bit of a change from the Spitfire-Messerschmitt series; but it did seem to me, not at the time perhaps, but certainly just afterwards, to be almost representative of what's happening to millions and millions of us. We're *all* on top of a foggy mountain, with slippery steep slopes on every side. A lot of the people who write to me remind me of my two impatient daughters. And curiously enough these people consist of two opposed classes. The first class cry "Yes, yes, yes, that's all right so far, but now work it out for us in detail, politically, economically, socially, this new order, this new world you mention," clean forgetting, of course, that my job here is to provide a seven-minute postscript to the Sunday night news bulletin, and not to give a four-hour lecture on all possible political, economic, and social developments.

The second class, who are equally impatient, and far more dangerous, say to me: "Look here, this won't do, you were all right when you started—funny bits, cheer-up stuff, Two-Ton Annie, all that. But now you're bringing ideas in—can't have that—danger to national unity—don't want ideas in war-time—no thinking— just working and fighting." But, of course, there couldn't be a more dangerous notion than this, not for this particular conflict, which isn't a war out of a serial story in the *Boys Own Paper*. It was ideas—or to be more exact, the absence of good ideas and the presence of bad ones—that brought into existence those vast armies and air forces against which we are fighting. They were created, largely by unscrupulous and indeed evil men, who themselves despaired of life, out of the bewilderment and despair of the people of Central Europe, who abandoned the search for a reasonable security, for a chance of equality, for the possibility of freedom. I agree that in the shadow of this vast menacing machine of destruction, we must work and we must fight as we have never worked and fought before, perhaps as no men and women have ever worked and fought before—but, to do this with a closed mind, content to repeat phrases that have lost all meaning and savour, not understanding what lies behind the immediate show of threat and terror, is to imprison ourselves in a colossal madhouse.

Therefore, I say, sometimes get clean away in mind and spirit from the whole thing, but then, when you return to it, don't be a mere cork bobbing about on a stream of information and rumour and dejected wonder, but cut through to the causes, the ideas. If a book or two will help you to make a start, I strongly recommend if you haven't read it, Peter Drucker's *The End of Economic Man*, which explains better than any book I know how the vast terrible idiocy of Nazism came to have such power, and what lies at the root of this world upheaval. You may not agree with all you read in this book *The End of Economic Man*—I don't myself—but at least it will help you to penetrate the bewildering shifting scene of tragic events, it will challenge your mind, it will set you thinking. You will still be on top of a mountain, in a thick fog, with steep slippery slopes all round, but the fog might lift a little and you might begin to catch a glimpse of a possible track, down into the valley, and the right valley, where there wait for you, there wait for us all somewhere, sometime, the friendly faces and bright fires of home.

Sunday, 1st September, 1940

THIS is the last Sunday of the first year of the War. I want to go back to-night to the first Sunday, the very first day of the War. I'll close my eyes and then wait to discover that Sunday of a year ago. It's a queer process, this hurrying through the blackout of the closed eyes, to find at the other side of this darkness the rich wonderland of memory, reflection, imagination. We call it "going inward", but surely the most inward world is the dense compact little world of our senses that's completely ruled by time. From that, we can only move outward; there's no other way. We can't retreat but must advance, in order to explore the vast golden globe of memory, reflection and imagination.

And now, here I am—it's that Sunday morning a year ago, and I am on my way up from the Isle of Wight, where I have been busy finishing a novel called *Let the People Sing*—yes, it was I who invented that phrase before the War—for it had been arranged weeks and weeks before that on Sunday, the 3rd of September, I should broadcast the first chapter of my novel, and they said they still wanted it in spite of the terrible news, so there I was, and it was an exquisite calm morning; the little voyage from Cowes to Southampton was pleasanter than usual, and the London road was very quiet, even for a Sunday morning.

Nearer London, down the long hill from Bagshot, there did seem to be rather a lot of heavily loaded cars passing us, but nothing happened until we entered the long narrow street of Staines. It was then, clean out of a quiet blue, that all the sirens screamed at us. Beneath the astonished noonday sun, people in steel helmets came hurrying, shouting and gesticulating. It was then I learned that we had been at war for the last hour. Caught by surprise in this crowded little town, jammed with people and cars, I must confess to having a moment of very real fear. As a civilian in the cheerful muddle of ordinary civilian life, surrounded by staring children and slow moving old folk, I didn't feel as I felt as a soldier; didn't know what might happen. I was for a moment terrified by the thought that it might be the worst I'd ever imagined, or, indeed, something unimaginable; a mumbling horror.

It is, of course, upon such fears, which are themselves the result of a newly won tenderness, a deepening piety, that the Dictators depend for most of their power. From the beginning they've carefully taken into account other people's affections and decencies, and have struck at the places from which a growing civilisation has removed the armour. It is for this reason that no talk of treaties, or economic injustices, can ever excuse them as persons, for they and all their kind recognise the goodness in others as a weakness to be profited by; a bared breast for their daggers, and if this isn't evil, then nothing is.

But no bombs fell that morning, and we continued our

journey into London, now a strange city of sandbags and shelters and first-aid posts. I knew then that the London I'd quitted so casually six weeks before had vanished for ever. Whatever might happen, I could never see that City again. It was at the end of one chapter of world history, while this strange City was at the beginning of another chapter.

Then, after packing some things I wanted at my Highgate house, in the middle of the afternoon, that hour so blank, colourless, tasteless on a hot Sunday, I rolled down through the long vacant roads of Kentish Town and Camden Town, which were as empty of life as old cities of the plague, into a Portland Place as quiet as a colour print, and then plunged, like another Alice down her rabbit hole, into Broadcasting House. There I seemed to have returned to the deep dugout life I'd once known among the chalk hills of the old French line. Down there the War was apparently in its second or third year. At any moment I felt I might be told to crawl out to a listening post, up towards Regent's Park. The tiny canteen where I had some tea was exactly like some frowsty Brigade Headquarters in the reserve line. The idea of reading my comic chapter into a microphone there now seemed more preposterous than ever.

But there, gasping and wheezing a little, I read it, as many of you probably remember.

I was making my exit from London that evening by train from Paddington, and I never remember seeing streets so empty before. It was like going in a taxi through an immense deserted film set of a city, still illuminated by great yellow lights. Through this unreality I carried within me a companion feeling of unreality, not unlike that I remember having on my way to a Nursing Home for an operation; a rather chill sense of a dreamlike state. This didn't survive my entrance into Paddington, which was crowded and looked as if it had had six consecutive Bank Holidays. History was being made, and as I suspect is usual when history is being made, the place reeked of weary humanity. The platforms were thick with wastepaper, half-eaten buns and empty bottles, and everywhere mothers appeared to be feeding their young. The trains you felt had no longer the old particular destinations. They were simply going and perhaps would never return.

As soon as my train pulled out, perhaps because although the train was crowded I happened to be alone, I was back again in that dreamlike state of mind. As we moved through the Western suburbs I stared up through the open window at the evening sky. Over in the west, hiding the dying sun, was the only patch of cloud to be seen, and it was shaped like a dragon. Do you remember that, any of you? Yes, a rampant dragon, etched in fire. The beast had been trapped inside the vast azure bowl. Against the exquisite fading blue, the barrage balloons glimmered like pearls, and they might have been a pattern of pearls, that had somehow been stitched on to the fabric of the evening sky. I don't ever remember seeing a nobler end to a day. It was the strings and clarinets and flutes bidding a high clear farewell to some lovely adagio. The light had grown unbelievably tender. How was it possible to believe that such a sky could spill ruin and death. It caught at the heart—that sky; not the heart that is entirely human and can go home and be content, but that other homeless heart we all possess, which even when there's no war, is never at peace, but dimly recognises that long ago it was conscripted for a bitter campaign and nameless battles in the snow. The train gathered speed; the Bowl of Heaven paled and expanded, and the dragon smouldered and then utterly faded.

There's no time to tell you now by what adventures I came that night to occupy the last bed in Basingstoke. But little good it did me I remember, for all the night the army lorries went roaring beneath my window, and sometimes I heard men singing, just as I'd gone singing through an autumn night five and twenty years before.

I'd time enough that night to wonder what was in store for us all; whether soon all our cities would be blazing, or there would be a long stalemate of huge entrenched armies. I never imagined then that before the next summer was over, Nazis would have swarmed like locusts, and have devoured like locusts, from Norway to the Pyrenees. And that the British Commonwealth alone would be defying both the Nazis and the Fascists, and not only defying them but answering blows with stouter blows. All that, and much more, was unforeseen, as I turned and wondered throughout that first night of the War.

But there was something that wasn't unforeseen, for I'd already written it down, and it has all come gloriously true. I guessed then what I have seen for myself since, and what I have told my overseas listeners more than once. The true heroes and heroines of this war, whose courage, patience and good humour stand like a rock above the dark morass of treachery, cowardice and panic, are the ordinary British folk. Talk about giving courage and confidence—you've given me more than I could ever give you; not only courage and confidence in the outcome of this war, but also faith in what we can all achieve after this war. Not only for ourselves but for decent men and women throughout the world, who all await the hour when the dragons will fade from the sky.

Sunday, 8th September, 1940

THERE are people who really enjoy being in danger. They fall in love with what seems to them its beautiful bright face. An immediate threat of destruction and death makes them feel more alive than they are at ordinary times. Danger wakes them up and gives the mere act of living a fine flavour. Now I'm not one of those people myself. I don't like being in danger. I've too much imagination, thank you. You can't live for years by using and developing your imagination without also becoming a rather apprehensive type of person. In my time I've been to a doctor to have some test or other, and in three seconds of his silence I've promptly given myself some frightful incurable disease, kept myself dying by inches, and then buried myself, to learn then that there was nothing the matter with me. Which ought to remind us, by the way, that we're always in danger, and that once past the age of twenty or so we know that the deaths we call violent, coming straight out of the blue, are the most merciful. But I'll admit that these noble reflections don't reconcile me to being in danger. I lived dangerously for long spells in the last war, and when that war was over I decided from then on I would be a comfortable pipe-and-slippers man and keep as close to cowardice as possible.

I mention these facts so that you'll understand, in what follows, that you're listening to a frail fellow citizen and not to one of these fire-eating heroes who occasionally find their way to the microphone. So when I talk of danger, I mean just what most of you mean, and I don't enjoy it. But like you, I try to carry on as cheerfully as I can, and don't do badly at it.

The fact that now we are nearly all at least within reach of danger seems to me one of the better and not one of the worse features of this war. I consider this an improvement on the last war, in which civilians, who developed some most unpleasant characteristics, lived in security while young men were mown down by the million. Twenty-five years ago we were preparing for the Battle of Loos, where on a six-mile front we had between fifty and sixty thousand casualties. This was good going but the following summer we did much better. On the 1st of July, 1916, there were whole towns in the north— my own amongst them—that lost at a stroke the fine flower of their young manhood. Almost every companion of my schooldays perished that morning. There never was such sudden terrible reaping. To have been a civilian then, sitting at ease while the telegrams arrived at every other house and the casualty lists grew and grew, must have been unendurable.

We are much better off now. At least we are sharing such danger as there is, and are not leaning back watching all our young men wither away. Strictly speaking, we're no longer civilians, and I think it was a pity that in the earlier months of this war the authorities were so emphatic that we *were* civilians, a helpless passive lot, so many skins to save, so much weight of tax-paying stuff to be huddled out of harm's way. We see now, when the enemy bombers come roaring at us at all hours, and it's our nerve *versus* his; that we're not really civilians any longer but a mixed lot of soldiers—machine-minding soldiers, milkmen and postmen soldiers, house-wife and mother soldiers—and what a gallant corps that is—and even broadcasting soldiers. Now and then, I feel, we ought to be paraded, and perhaps a few medals handed out. Two days ago, an oldish man came to see me about an inventory, for he was employed by an estate agent, and he mentioned mildly at the end of the meeting that he was still feeling rather disturbed because a few days before a bomb had arrived in his front garden and brought the whole house down on the little sitting-room where he and his wife were taking shelter, and they had had to be taken out of the wreckage. And there he was, homeless himself, coolly going through our inventory. Yes, I think a few medals would do no harm.

We haven't, of course, quite settled down yet to this soldier-civilian life; we haven't all adopted the same technique, and there are wild differences of opinion. I've been noticing these differences all this last week because some workmen have been doing a very necessary job outside my house, and I haven't been able to avoid overhearing their heated arguments. These chaps repre-sented all the familiar attitudes. One man insisted on working on during the alarms and roundly declared, in my hearing, that anybody who went off to a shelter was no better than a Fifth Columnist—in fact, *was* a so-and-so Fifth Columnist, which seemed to me a bit severe.

Another, at the opposite extreme of opinion, legged it for a shelter as soon as he heard the sirens. The other two, like most of us, avoided these extremes, and now tried this way and now tried that. It's a good thing, by the way, during these weeks of battle—for that is what they are, and we're all in it—to take a very tolerant line about differences of opinion, to remember that we're all fellow soldiers, to make *more* and not less allowance than usual for the astonishing queerness of other folk, to be more polite and considerate and, indeed downright friendly than ever before, just because we *are* sharing a battle. It would do us no harm to imagine that everybody we meet during the day, even if it is only to buy or sell some little thing, has been encountered in the smoke and fury of the battlefield.

After all, you know, just now we're not really obscure persons tucked away in our offices and factories, villas and back streets; we're the British people being attacked and fighting back; we're in the great battle for the future of our civilisation; and so instead of being obscure and tucked away, we're bang in the middle of the world's stage with all the spotlights focused on us; we're historical personages, and it's possible that distant generations will find inspiration, when their time of trouble comes, in the report in their history books of our conduct at this hour; just as it is certain that our airmen have already found a shining place for ever in the world's imagination, becoming one of those bands of young heroes, creating a saga, that men can never forget.

I do a great deal of broadcasting in the small hours to the Dominions and the United States, and these talks which go out on short wave, are picked up by little groups of our own folk all over the world, at the very ends of the earth—as I know from messages—from the heart of Africa to the far Straits of Magellan. These talks bring me many cables and letters from those distant listening folk, to whom I describe as best I can how all you people at home are facing each new ordeal, how nobly you've responded to every call, how when the whole waiting world was afraid, your spirits rose and rose to a magnificent defiance. Well, I wish you could read these letters I receive, from the Dominions, from all over the United States, and, most moving of all, from tiny groups, often just a man and wife, of British folk far, far away, perhaps high in the Andes or on some tropical island. And I wish you could understand with what deep anxiety, and now with what renewed hope, with what pride and joy, what smiles and tears, they listen to our accounts of you and of this glorious new chapter in our island history. Danger! Why?—and remember, I speak as a comfortable pipe-and-slippers man, none of your heroes but a wary, and, you might almost say, cowardly old soldier, a lead-swinger, a dodger of the column—but why, I repeat, what's a bit of danger compared with such pride and joy and trust? Good night.

Sunday, 15th September, 1940

THERE is no evidence to suggest that Herr Hitler and Marshal Goering are well-read in English literature, and I should doubt if they ever spent much time with *Pickwick Papers*. But their attention ought to be drawn to Chapter ten of that immortal work, in which chapter Samuel Weller makes his first appearance.

He was, if you remember, cleaning boots in the yard of the White Hart Inn, when a smart chambermaid called over the balustrade of the gallery, "Sam;" "Hello", replied Sam. "No. 22 wants his boots." Sam replied: "Ask 22 whether he'll have them now or wait till he gets 'em." "Come, don't be a fool, Sam," said the girl coaxingly, "the gentleman wants his boots directly." "Well, you are a nice young 'ooman for a musical party, you are," said Sam. "Look at these 'ere boots; eleven pair of boots, and one shoe as belongs to No. 6 with a wooden leg. The eleven boots is to be called at half-past eight and the shoe at nine. Who's No. 22 that's to put all the others out. No, no, 'regular rotation,' as Jack Ketch said when he tied the man up. 'Sorry to keep you a-waiting, Sir, but I'll attend to you directly'."

That's Sam Weller, and there seems to me nearly all the true cockney spirit, independence, ironic humour, cheek and charm shown in that tiny bit of dialogue.

A lot of us, especially if we are from the North, and thought we knew everything, imagined that that old cockney spirit was dead and gone. We thought the Londoner of to-day, catching his tubes and electric trains, was a different kind of fellow altogether, with too many of his corners rubbed off, too gullible, easily pleased, too soft; and we were wrong. This last grim week has shown us how wrong we were. The Londoners, as the Americans are saying, can take it, and London itself—this grey sea of a city—can take it. The fact that the savage indiscriminate bombing of the city has seized the world's imagination, is itself a tribute to the might and majesty of London. There was a time when, like many north-countrymen who came South, I thought I disliked London; it had vast colourless suburbs that seemed to us even drearier than the ones we had left behind. We hated the extremes of wealth and poverty that we found, cheek by jowl in the West End, where at night the great purring motor-cars filled with glittering women passed the shadowy rows of the homeless, the destitute, the down-and-out.

The life here in London seemed to us to have less colour, less gaiety then life in capitals abroad, and at the same time to have less character and flavour than the life we remembered in our provincial cities. And so on and so forth. But on these recent nights, when I have gone up to high roofs and have seen the fires like open wounds on the vast body of the city, I've realised, like many another settler here, how deeply I've come to love London, with its misty, twilit charm, its hidden cosiness and companionship, its smoky magic. The other night, when a few fires were burning so fiercely, that half the sky was aglow, and the tall terraces around Portland Place were like pink palaces in the Arabian Nights, I saw the Dome and Cross of St. Paul's, silhouetted in sharpest black against the red flames and orange fumes, and it looked like an enduring symbol of reason and Christian ethics seen against the crimson glare of unreason and savagery. "Though giant rains put out the sun, here stand I for a sign."

In a supreme battle for the world's freedom, there can be no doubt that you and I are now in the midst of such a battle, there are only two capital cities in the world that are worthy of figuring in its portrait—one of them is Paris, city of quick barricades and revolutions, now temporarily out of the fight, not because its brave people lost heart but rather because they lost interest and so allowed banal men, intriguers greedy for wealth and power and all the enemies of a people on the march, to deceive and betray them.

The other city is great London, which during the last thousand years—and what are the wobblings and timidities of the last ten years compared with the nine hundred and ninety that went before—has many a time given itself a shake and risen to strike a blow for freedom, and not only its own freedom but that of men everywhere. In this capacity, as any European history book will show you, it is in sharp contrast to Berlin which has never yet been regarded as a beacon light by the free spirit of mankind. But London has often been seen as such a beacon light. Even the chief revolutionaries of our time lived here in their day and were nourished on books paid for by London citizens. And now, in the darkest hour, it blazes again; yes, because the incendiary bombs have been rained upon it but also because its proud defiance and unconquerable spirit have brought to men and women all over the world renewed hope and courage.

This, then, is a wonderful moment for us who are here in London, now in the roaring centre of the battlefield, the strangest army the world has ever seen, an army in drab civilian clothes, doing quite ordinary things, an army of all shapes and sizes and ages of folk, but nevertheless a real army, upon whose continuing high and defiant spirit the world's future depends.

Much has been made, both here and overseas, of the fine courage and resolution of the London citizen, and especially of all the people in the various air-raid services, and our most inspiring voice, that of the Prime Minister, has told us of our high destiny. But I venture to think that not enough has been made of two facts. First, that we are not civilians who have happened to stray into a kind of hell on earth, but that we are soldiers fighting a battle. And this isn't a mere figure of speech and shouldn't be regarded as such, because I am certain it would be wiser to treat persons doing essential work in certain areas on a military basis, removing all people not doing essential work from such areas and providing the rest, the front-line troops of our battle of London, with all necessary shelter, food and transport.

Some of us said long before this blitzkrieg began that the pretence that life was more or less normal for everybody was a very dangerous one. It's better to say outright, now we're all going to have a jolly good shake up, but only in order to carry on all the better. Most people don't mind that—they rather like it, but, of course, nobody likes being bombed at all odd hours; to go home as I did the other morning at dawn and notice that a large bus has been flattened like a tin toy against the second storey of a building, is to feel, to say the least of it, that things are becoming most rum and peculiar. Which brings me to the second fact that's been under-stressed. It is that we have not suddenly entered upon a new and quite lunatic way of living with the prospect of months and months and months of sirens and shelters and bombs before us (which is what some authorities appear to imagine), but that we have been flung into a battle—a real terrific honest-to-God battle—perhaps the most important this war will see, and that, therefore, we must summon up all the courage and resolution and cheerful-ness we possess and stick it out until the battle is over. As a kind of civilian life this is hellish, but as battles go, it is not at all bad—with some shelter, meals arriving fairly regularly and a quick rescue of the wounded. But I am not giving this advice to the cockneys—they don't need any from me, only an apology for ever imagining their old spirit had left them, and a stare of admiration. They can say to Herr Hitler and Marshal Goering (who really will have to read *Pickwick*) what Sam Weller said: "Sorry to keep you waiting, Sir, but I'll attend to you directly."

Sunday, 22nd September, 1940

THIS ought to be a very special postscript—I don't mean specially good, though it would be very nice if it were; but special in its appeal, for it's about women and the war—so that half my listeners are hearing about themselves (which always has a fascination) and the other half (my half—the lads, the men, the chaps) are hearing something about the mysterious opposite sex (which has always had a certain charm, too).

Now I'll begin boldly by admitting that in my own attitude towards women there is a mixture—an uneasy mixture—of fine dashing male contempt and half-secret respect, and even fear. I must add that I share these feelings with about 750 million other males. This gives a liberal allowance extending to several hundred million males for those mistaken fellows whose attitude is all contempt or all fear.

The contempt we feel is explained by the fact that women seem to us to be taken in by all kinds of bits of nonsense that wouldn't deceive us for two seconds. On the other hand, our respect and our fear arise from our knowledge that rubbishy stuff that takes us in has no chance whatever with the realistic and clear-sighted and strangely tenacious female mind. They see clean through it at a glance.

Now there's a familiar type of masculine mind that believes that women should have nothing to do with political and public life. Woman's place, they tell us, is in the home. It's largely the same mind, I believe, that then muddles away so that the home is put on short rations and then bombed. Privately I've believed for years the opposite of this—that a great deal of political and public life is nothing but large-scale common-sense housekeeping, and that as women have an almost terrifying amount of common-sense and the ones who are good at housekeeping are very good at it, then the sooner some of our communal and national affairs are managed by women the better.

The same kind of man would say at once that women would make a mess of it; to which we can retort that it would be hard to make a bigger mess than men have made during the last twenty-five years, culminating in the world-wide idiocy of to-day.

Moreover, please notice this, that where all the worst mischief has been started women have had the least say in affairs. For example, high finance and big business have not exactly played a brilliant part in our life during these last years, and it's well known that women are entirely unfit to intervene in these matters. Then we know that the Nazis and the Fascists from the first swept aside all thought of co-operation with their womenfolk, whom they regarded as mere breeding stock or toys to amuse the tired warrior.

You can easily imagine that there weren't any women in Germany and Italy—no wondering, suffering,

sorrowing mothers, wives, sisters, sweethearts—nothing
but trampling, bragging, swaggering, idiotic males, silly
little boys who've somehow grown to be the size of men.
You'd have thought, too, that at the mere first sight of the
neurotic, screaming Hitler and of his gang of toughs that
all the women would have risen in instant revolt and
have cried that such men were unfit to control the
destiny of even one single schoolboy. That they didn't is
our tragedy—resulting in a war that seems to me to hit
harder at women than it does at men. For this is total
war; and total war is war right inside the home itself,
emptying the clothes cupboards and the larder, screaming its threats through the radio at the hearth, burning
and bombing its way from roof to cellar. It's ten times
harder being a decent housewife and mother during such
a war than it is being a soldier. You have to make a far
greater effort to keep going, for you've no training and
discipline to armour you. The soldier has his own
responsibilities, but when he assumed them he was
released from a great many others; whereas his women-
folk know no such release, but have more and more
responsibility piled upon them.

And they needn't even be wives and mothers. Nothing
has impressed me more in this bombing battle of London
than the continued high courage and resolution, not only
of the wives and mothers but also of the crowds of nurses,
secretaries, clerks, telephone girls, shop assistants, wait-
resses, who morning after morning have turned up for
duty neat as ever—rather pink about the eyes, perhaps,
and smiling rather tremulously, but still smiling.

Here's this big bully, Goering, who for six years has been

given all the resources of Germany to create the most terrible and merciless weapon of oppression Europe had ever known—the German air force; and he arrives in Northern France to command it himself, and to tell it to do its worst; and there are launched all the thunderbolts of the new Teutonic fury, and the whole world holds its breath. And what happens? Why, a lot of London girls—pale-faced little creatures living on cups of tea and buns, who go tripping from tiny villas and flats with their minute attache-cases to Tubes and buses and then to offices and shops—defy this Goering and all his Luftwaffe and all their high explosives and incendiaries and machine-guns—and successfully defy them, still trotting off to work, still carrying on, still trim and smiling. Isn't that a triumph?

I've just had a message from an American friend, concluding with this cry: "What a great race you are!" But I shall tell him that our men wouldn't be so fine if our women at this fateful hour were not so magnificent. There isn't an airman, submarine commander, or unnamed hero in a bomb squad who hasn't behind him at least one woman, and perhaps half a dozen women, as heroic as himself. Not that everybody rises at once, of course, to the heights—there are bad gaps in the roll of honour; for instance, spending an odd night in a village where my own womenfolk were busy trying to arrange for the billeting of mothers and babies who've been bombed out of the East End, I was shocked to learn that some middle-class women in that neighbourhood, with any amount of room to spare in their houses, made every excuse to avoid receiving any of these mothers and babies.

I feel sure that if such women had been in London lately they would have soon changed their minds—which perhaps lack imagination rather than goodwill. But if they know—and still don't care—then they ought to be ashamed of themselves. It means they belong still to the world that's brought itself, and us, into this hell of senseless destruction and suffering—a world of cold narrow minds, of greed, privilege and love of power. And we're fighting not merely to keep the German jackboot off our necks but also to put an end once and for all to that world, and to bring into existence an order of society in which nobody will have far too many rooms in a house and nobody have far too few.

And all wondering, suffering women—some of them homeless, lost, with bewildered small children in their arms—should be told here and now that that is what we're all struggling and battling for. Not for some re-grouping on the chess-board of money and power politics; but for new and better homes—real homes—a decent chance at last—new life. And every woman should remember that—keep the promise locked in her heart, and when the time comes, with one voice—and, if necessary, with that full feminine fury which is among the most awe-inspiring phenomenon—demand that the promise be redeemed, so that the children now hurried through the shelters can one day walk in the sunlight and build upon our ruins a glorious new world.

Sunday, 29th September, 1940

PERHAPS the only solidly real place we ever know is the place in which we spent our childhood and youth. It's there there are genuinely real streets, squares, shops and houses, and their only fault is that they have a trick, like the queer cards that conjurers sometimes use, of appearing diminished every time we go back to have another look at them.

I was thinking this when I returned the other afternoon to my native city of Bradford, where I went to see what damage had resulted from a recent air-raid. And, as I anticipated, it was far more of a shock to see a few burnt-out buildings in this town than it had been to see all the damage in London. It was astonishing to discover that the familiar large drapery store and the old chapel were no longer there, and that in their places were some blackened ruins with odd pillars and bits of walls still standing, which had an unexpectedly dignified look about them; not the now familiar ignoble and now almost obscene sight of bombed buildings, with their pitiful broken rafters and motionless cataracts of debris, but rather picturesque ruins with a hint of Pompeii or Herculaneum about them. But I think the sight made a far deeper impression upon me than all the bombing I had seen for weeks and weeks in London, because it somehow brought together two entirely different worlds; the safe and shining world of my childhood, and this insecure and lunatic world of to-day, so it caught and held my imagination. I was appalled by the sheer stupidity of it; these Nazi airmen had flown hundreds and hundreds of miles in order to destroy a draper's shop, part of a cinema and a market, an old chapel, and so on; nothing that made the least difference to our war effort, nothing that couldn't be soon replaced—except, of course, the old walls of the chapel. Even already the drapers have taken other premises, the market's open, and I've no doubt that the congregation of the old chapel has found hospitality, if perhaps an inferior brand of sermon, at other places of worship.

Moreover—and now we come to the point—the pie-shop and the pie were still there. I must explain about these. Ever since I could remember there'd been just at the back of this draper's a small eating-house that specialised in meat and potato pie; one of those little Dickensy places that still survive in provincial towns. I remembered it well, though I was never one of its customers, because there'd always been on view in the window, to tempt the appetite of the passer-by, a giant, almost superhuman, meat and potato pie with a magnificently brown, crisp, artfully wrinkled, succulent looking crust. And not only that—and now we approach the marvellous, the miraculous—out of that pie there came at any and every hour when the shop was doing business, a fine rich appetising steam to make the mouth water even as the very window itself was watering.

There it was, a perpetual volcano of a meat and potato pie.

And that steaming giant pie was to my boyish mind—and, indeed, to my adult mind, for we never forget these things—as much an essential part of my native city as the Town Hall and its chimes.

Now, I'd heard that this shop and its famous steaming pie had been destroyed in the raid, and so when I went to see what had happened, I'd made up my mind that I would stand in the ruins of that shop, catching perhaps a last faint lingering whiff of that steam, and would compose some kind of lament or elegy. But, I found that the shop hadn't finished, but was there, wide open, and doing business. True, it was showing a few scars, and instead of the window, it had been neatly boarded up, but there was a square opening in the middle of the painted boarding and there, seen through the opening, framed perhaps a little narrowly but in itself as magnificent as ever, was the great pie, still brown, crisp, succulent, and steaming away like mad. Every puff and jet of that steam defied Hitler, Goering, and the whole gang of them. It was glorious.

Now, the owner himself, an elderly man with one of those "folded-in" Yorkshire faces, and character written all over him, was standing just inside the doorway. So I asked him, in my delight and relief, what had happened. He replied shortly, and, indeed, rather grumpily, that the shop had had its front blown out but was now open, as I could see, and that the famous pie hadn't been damaged at all, because it was his habit when closing the shop to remove this noble trade-mark to a place of safety. As he said this I could feel his hand on my back and a distinct sensation of being gently but firmly pushed into the street, where, the hand hinted, I belonged. Rather grieved by this suspicious reception, I went further along to have a closer look at the neighbouring ruins. I had not been there more than a minute or two before I was clapped on the shoulder, and there was the pie-man again, this time wearing his coat and not wearing his apron, holding out a hand and beaming at me. It seems that his wife recognised my voice. I am not telling this for my own glory, though I must say it's one of the most handsome compliments I ever received. And so after doing a quick change with his apron and coat, he came round after me. He didn't admit as much; indeed, we never went into the question, but I think that he'd imagined that I was some trade rival—no doubt I have a look of the younger ambitious pie-man about me —who was anxious to discover after years of unsuccessful fifth-column work the secret of the famous steaming pie.

Now, this secret was revealed to me, without my even asking, by its owner, all smiles and friendship and confidence, but, of course, I can't pass it on to all you people, but I will say this: that suspicions I'd entertained ever since the age of fourteen about that giant pie, for ever jetting forth its fragrant steam, were now amply confirmed. "Ai," said the pie-man proudly, "it's a secret, that pie is, and a rare lot 'ud like to know how it's done. I've had it five and forty years, that same pie, and luckily I'd put it away in a good safe place same as usual, so as soon as we got started again, and we wasn't long I can tell you, and I get's window boarded up, I got pie out again. There's only one thing," he added wistfully, "that 'ole I'd left in the centre of the boarding to see the pie through. Ai, well, it's not quite big enough." I wanted to tell him that that was a national fault of ours. We have the pie, and nobody's going to take it from us, but we do have a habit of boarding it up a bit too closely, and we need to open out and to give the people a better look at the pie, and give the pie a better sight of the people.

And now, I suppose, all my more severe listeners are asking each other why this fellow has to go on yapping about his pies and nonsense at a time like this when the whole world is in a turmoil, the fate of empires is in the balance, and men, women and children are dying terrible violent deaths; to which I can only reply, that we must keep burnished the bright little thread of our common humanity that still runs through these iron days and black nights; and that we are fighting to preserve and, indeed, I hope to enlarge that private and all-important little world of our own reminiscence and humour and homely poetry in which a pie that steamed for forty-five years and successfully defied an air-raid to steam again has its own proper place.

Sunday, 6th October, 1940

THE other evening I was going by car down the western side of England, on my way to do a certain job. I was being driven by an engineer in the employ of a well-known public corporation. It was an unpleasant evening, chilly, damp, with rain threatening, and dusk coming far too early. It seemed as if winter was only just round the corner. This may explain why our talk along the road was more grim than gay. The engineer grumbled because his subsistence allowance was now less than it had been before the war, having been reduced by some strange officials who imagined that prices would be less in wartime. I grumbled at the evening and said I'd rather be faced with a desperate war in summer than any kind of war in winter. He said that travelling, which he had to do continually, was a wearing game these days for sometimes it took him an hour or two at the end of a long day to find any sort of bed. I replied, with my eye on the sad, early dusk, conjuring up thoughts of a 4.30 blackout, that now was the time for our leaders to use a little imagination, to light beacons in this gathering darkness, to warm our hearts and set fire to our minds, by proclaiming noble and universal aims; by so ordering affairs in this country that we might serve as an example to the world, not merely in courage and endurance, but in bold and hopeful planning for the future, releasing in us great creative forces. Just a little imagination, that's all, I added. My companion, a sceptic, said he hoped we'd see it. I said that I hoped we would, too; and by this time the last glimmer of daylight had vanished, and we were crawling through a rainy darkness. I said we'd better stop at the next town and put up for the night. The engineer said that it would be a good idea to *start* trying to find beds at the next town. We arrived there— nothing to be seen, of course—but I knew which it was and remembered it as being a pretty little place. We were told that of the three hotels there only one had been left open to the public, so we went to that one, where I enquired for two rooms; or at least two beds. This seemed to amuse them; no beds to be had there. I gathered, though it wasn't exactly mentioned, that there wouldn't be vacant rooms there for months. So I tele- phoned to other hotels further along our route and they laughed merrily, too, and hinted that they had been full for weeks and would remain full for months. I said that there appeared to be a surprising number of people travelling in these rather out-of-the-way parts, and was told that all these guests weren't travellers, but resident guests; people who had settled in these hotels to be out of the way of sirens and anti-aircraft guns, and bombs. Well, that was all right. Nobody in their senses wants a noisy night in a shelter if a quiet night in bed is to be had at all; though this arrangement did seem rather tough luck on all those people who have to be travelling about the country on what might be urgent business.

G

Eventually, through the personal attention of one landlord, we did manage to obtain a room and a couple of beds, and were able to say good-bye to the black, dripping road.

It was after that, and after comparing notes with several knowledgeable persons, that I began to meditate, sombrely, perhaps being influenced by the night, on one of the smaller ironies of this war here; and it's this, that a large proportion of the people who are able to live in comparative peace, security and quiet, consists, not of persons recovering from overwork, strain or shock, but those persons who don't know what to do with themselves. I don't say for a moment that it's their fault. Many of them no doubt have tried, over and over again, to find some useful wartime occupation before settling into these remote and charming places; and, so far as this is the case, they are to be pitied and not envied. Some of them have been made to feel useless, first by stupid parents, and afterwards by a badly organised community, all their lives.

This has, for a long time now, been a country in which there are far too many pleasant, able-bodied persons who, because of some system of private incomes or pensions and all kinds of snobbish nonsense, are condemned to yawn away their lives, forever wondering what to do between meals; in startling contrast to the other people who wonder how to get it all done between meals.

This is undoubtedly true of certain types of women, who have been made so comfortably secure by timid parents that they have been shut out of the whole adventure of living. The bitterest letters I have received during these past few months, have not been from men, piloting fighters or bombers, or stoking minesweepers, or from women nursing under fire, or looking after evacuated babies, but from ladies doing nothing in inland resorts, where their energy is all turned inward instead of outward, turning into hostility instead of into helpfulness and fun.

So don't think I'm blaming anybody personally. But the situation is, you must admit, rather peculiar. It's as if you went to one hospital in a town and found most of the beds occupied by people who had nothing to do and thought they would have an afternoon's snooze. And if at the same time in this town you found scores of injured persons lying about the pavement, you might reasonably come to the conclusion that things were badly managed in that town. Well, of course, we don't have injured persons lying about the pavement for long. But, on the other hand, I do seem to have heard of and, indeed, to have seen, a great many mothers and children from badly bombed areas who have been got away but not, so to speak, anywhere in particular, certainly not to nice, quiet rooms in pretty places where they might quickly recover from recent shocks. And some of them I am afraid have been regarded as a nuisance, which is just like treating a trainload of wounded soldiers as a nuisance. I am not blaming anybody—I really don't know if anybody *is* to blame; but all this, with many more unpleasant little ironies besides, does suggest that, for all our grand, vague talk, we are at present floundering between two stools. One of them is our old acquaintance labelled 'Every man for himself, and the devil take the hindmost', which can't really represent us or else why should young men, for whom you and I have done little or nothing, tear up and down the sky in their Spitfires to protect us, or why should our whole community pledge itself to fight until Europe is freed.

The other stool, on which millions are already perched without knowing it, has some lettering round it that hints that free men could combine, without losing what's essential to their free development, to see that each gives according to his ability, and receives according to his need. That aspiration, which might have come from the merest and mildest sermon, used to shock our fathers and grandfathers, but we—who've seen a thousand things that would have shocked them still more, who've seen all hell let loose because men refuse to think properly and feel decently, are now being hammered into sterner stuff, and may even consider, before we've done, letting Sunday's sentiments spill over into Monday's arrangements, and acting out a mild sermon or two; and so prove that not only when we say we'll fight, we'll fight— which we have already done to the great astonishment of the Nazi leaders—but also that what we say we are fighting for is the very thing for which we are fighting; that here, at least, is no mere propaganda but the blazing truth of the mind and heart.

Sunday, 13th October, 1940

A LISTENER began his letter to me the other day by saying "I think we're very much alike; we're about the same age, and both short and plump, though you, I think, are more so." Well, as a Yorkshireman, I think my own folk and those of Lancashire—where I have been spending this last week—are very much alike, but the Lancashire folk are more so.

If, as the Prime Minister told us, we must now be both "grim and gay", then Lancashire will come out all right, for its people have always been very grim and very gay, except of course when they try to play cricket against Yorkshire, when they are only very grim.

I suggested myself some weeks ago that we might take as our motto now "Hard work and high jinks". That has always been the motto of Lancashire, whether holiday-making at Blackpool, it seems as determined, noisy and ruthless as the cotton-spinning and weaving at Salford or Blackburn. It's no secret that we're now having some air-raids up here. The other night I found myself out in the open street, almost keeping an appointment with a Molotov bread-basket. If the tactics of Marshal Goering have failed elsewhere in Britain—as we know they have—you may be sure that that star-spangled thug hasn't a dog's chance in these parts. I hope, though, that the widest publicity will be given to the new Nazi reasons for this indiscriminate bombing, as frankly stated over the air by their heroic friends in Rome. Hitler's purpose, it seems, in blowing up or setting fire to Churches, Chapels, Children's Hospitals and Old Men's Homes is to shake our nerves and set our consciences to work so that we will rebel against our present leaders. Apparently, when enough Children's Hospitals and Old Men's Homes have been destroyed, we shall all rise as one man and demand to be ruled by prominent Fifth Columnists chosen by the nice, kind gentlemen in Germany, who no doubt shed a tear every time they learn that their air-force has wrecked a few more cottages, just as no doubt they shed a tear after their famous week-end of the long knives, when they murdered in cold blood about half their former comrades. We can no more understand such people than they can understand us; we appear to live in two different worlds. It's a great pity that Dictators, whose popularity is so overwhelming that they can only travel in armoured trains, can't move about as the rest of us are able to do, to learn for themselves what other people are really like instead of depending upon the lying reports of secret agents.

For example, a day in a cotton mill, such as I have had this week, would have given them some valuable information about the real English people. Perhaps, if Herr von Ribbentrop, during his fateful stay in this country, had had a few hours' frank talk with some overlookers or miners, he might have learned a few things impossible to discover in Carlton House Terrace.

The gaiety, which is here still, though it may seem to outsiders to take strange form, might have eluded him, but I think that the moment he began stamping and screaming, he'd have noticed the grimness all right. But even in these parts, where they are as toughly determined to enjoy themselves as they are not to be bullied by anybody, I feel that now that autumn is with us, and the shadow of winter already darkening the horizon, some official assistance will soon be urgently needed to make certain that this gaiety has some communal outlet; in other words, recreation and entertainment should be planned and organised. We mustn't allow ourselves to be reduced to living on an ever-narrowing edge of war-time existence, with nothing to think about but planes and tanks and guns. The gayer and richer the life we have to defend the more anxious we shall be to defend it. Noble words finely spoken, great music, all the treasures of art, laughter and lights, and song, these mustn't be banished but should be given a greater place than ever before in our lives. This winter, here in Lancashire, everything from the Hallé Orchestra pealing out the finale of Brahm's Fourth Symphony, to a bit of clog dancing should be in full swing. All the graces of life should be discovered in public, as well as in private; I say in private, because just now it seems to me that it's among the byways and the humble folk who live in them, that you see and hear things that give you renewed hope and confidence in our species, which in its dealings among its large-scale organisations, its military Empires and nation States, appears to behave as if it knew nothing but greed, cunning, violence, hate and idiocy. The War Lord at the top behaves as if he were a drunken caveman. He meets another of his sort, each guarded as if he were a precious relic, and together —surrounded by figures who might have come out of the pageant of the Seven Deadly Sins—they squint suspiciously at each other and plot new treacheries to the human race.

Meanwhile, far below, among the decent common folk, the graces and courtesies of life still flourish. The other day, in a north-western city—no, we've had enough of that, it was in Liverpool—I heard of a woman who keeps a small café in one of the main streets. We'll call her, as so many of her patrons have done, just "Ma". When the boys came back from Dunkirk Ma would ask them into her café to have some tea or coffee, and to try her home-made scones, and somehow would contrive to forget the bill. Then some sailors from the French Fleet arrived in the city, and were to be seen wandering about, bewildered and wistful, and she managed to convey to these foreign sailors that if they'd no money—most of them hadn't for a time—it was all the same to her—the café was open to them. Then one day, three of these French sailors, having just enjoyed her coffee and cakes, were terribly embarrassed because they had no money to pay for them, and nothing to offer in return but thanks in a strange tongue. Was there nothing they could give? There was; they whipped off the bands from their hats inscribed with *Marine Nationale*, and presented them to her, and a few days later the middle-aged proprietress of a café might have been seen wearing a Marine Nationale band round her hair to the delight of all patrons, and especially all the foreign ones. This is, of course, a thoroughly subversive anecdote. Disciplinary action ought to have been taken all round; we can't have that sort of thing going on or military discipline would soon be reduced to a mere farce; except, of course, that if there had been more of that sort of thing, more pleasant, easy, friendly giving and taking, more of the graces and courtesies of life, not only at the bottom, among the humble folk, but also bang at the top, among the great ones, among the very nations themselves, then all military discipline could be reduced to a farce and it wouldn't matter a brass farthing. If a hundredth part of the goodwill and sense shown at the little café round the corner were imported into our international affairs; if greed, ingratitude and treachery were regarded as vices in great conferences, just as they are in pubs, then all these chest-thumping, screaming lunatics, and all their insane paraphernalia of destruction, would vanish like the figures and furnishings of some bad dream; as, indeed, very soon they will.

Sunday, 20th October, 1940

THIS is my last Sunday postscript for some time, perhaps the last I shall ever do. The decision was mine and was in no way forced upon me by the B.B.C. My relations with the B.B.C. are excellent. But I had some good reasons for wanting to stop; in the first place people get tired of hearing the same voice at exactly the same time each week, and I'd be the last man to want to add to the boredom and tedium of this war. I've always pleaded for more imagination in the handling of the war; more flags and less red tape; more music and fun, hard work and high jinks, and the least I can do when I am in danger of becoming one of the war bores myself, is to get out and so make a little change for you even if it's only on Sundays at 9.15.

Then again, there's another rather more subtle reason for having a change of talker on Sunday nights, and it's this. That the whole situation of the country and also the mood of the country have changed, and so it might be better if these were interpreted for you on Sundays by another speaker. As many of you will remember, I began these postscripts just after Dunkirk; got going with them during those blazing summer weeks when France collapsed and we were threatened with immediate invasion, and world opinion began to think we were doomed. We knew very well that we weren't doomed, and our people began to show the world what stuff they're made of, and the sight was glorious.

Throughout those weeks as the spirits of the British people rose, to the bewilderment and secret concern of the Nazis, who couldn't understand such behaviour, many of us felt that here now was a country capable, not only of defying and then defeating the Nazis and Fascists, but capable too of putting an end to the world that produced Nazis and Fascists; capable of working a miracle, the miracle of man's liberation.

That was the high mood of the summer and I can only hope that I went some little way towards expressing it. Certainly it was a great privilege to be allowed to make the attempt. As I told you once before, when so many of you wrote to say I gave you courage and hope, I wanted to explain that it was you who gave me courage and hope, the truth being, I suppose, that we all gave each other courage and hope, like members of a sensible, affectionate family.

Now this period, I think, came to an end with the defeat of the German Air Force over England by the R.A.F. and the failure of Goering's terror tactics to break the morale of the people of London. We're now entering a new period, and I think it should be interpreted to you on Sunday nights by a new postscripter, and preferably a speaker who feels the same exultation about this period that I did about the earlier one. I admit that I don't, partly no doubt because five months of broadcasting late at night on the Overseas service have left me feeling increasingly tired, but there are other reasons. Let me say at once that these have nothing to do with the general war situation, which is, of course, far more favourable to us than it was during the summer. But the high generous mood, so far as it affects our destinies here, is vanishing with the leaves. It is as if the poets had gone and the politicians were coming back.

Stupid persons have frequently accused me in public of—I use their own words—taking advantage of my position to bring party politics into my talks. This is extremely ironical because I am not a member of any political party. I've no close personal relations with any prominent members of any party, and no expectations from the success of any particular party, whereas it is obvious that these critics of mine are members of a political party and that their criticism comes from taking a narrow party line. It's not I, but they, who put party before country, for I've never even learnt to think in terms of a political party. And the most I've asked for in these talks is that we should mean what we say; be really democratic, for example, while fighting for democracy; and that we should make some attempt to discover the deeper causes of this war and to try and find a remedy for them, thus making this a colossal battle, not only against something, but also for something positive and good. If all this, together with certain obvious elements of social justice and decency seems to you Socialism, Communism or Anarchy, then you are at liberty to call me a Socialist, a Communist or an Anarchist, though I would implore you to stop merely pasting on labels and instead to think a little.

There's a danger that as this high mood passes, apathy will return to some sections of the community and selfishness and stupidity to some other sections. Bear with me, those of you who disagree, for a last minute or two, while I try and explain as briefly as possible what I feel about this country and this war.

I think it's true to say that at the present time this country of ours, because of its courage and its proud defiance, its determination to put an end to this international brigandage and racketeering of the Hitlers and Mussolinis and their riff-raff is the hope of all that is best in the world, which watches us with admiration. But our greatest potential ally is not this power or that, but the growing hope in decent folk everywhere that civilisation can be saved, or, should I say, the seeds of civilisation could be saved to take root and to flower afterwards; that a reasonable liberty along with a reasonable security can be achieved; that democracy is not an experiment that was tried and that failed, but a great creative force that must now be released again. If we can make all these things plain to the world by the way in which we now order our lives here, then I don't believe this will even be a long war—the daylight will come soon and all these evil apparitions from the night of men's bewilderment and despair will vanish, but if apathy and stupidity return to reign once more; if the privileges of a few are seen to be regarded as more important than the happiness of many; if a sterile obstruction is preferred to creation; if our faces are still turned towards the past instead of towards the future; if too many of us will simply not trouble to know, or if we do know, will not care, then the great opportunity will pass us by, and soon the light will be going out again.

For this reason I make no apology to those listeners who, out of their impregnable fortresses of stupidity, have assured me of their hostility. I can only assure them that I propose to go on disliking more and more everything they stand for. To all the other listeners—a very large majority—I can offer whichever they prefer, apologies or thanks; apologies if they found a North-country accent is irritating or wearying, as some of us find other accents; if they wearied of me talking about myself, though sometimes the most honest way of discussing general topics is to be personal about them; if they became impatient because I couldn't—as I obviously couldn't—convert a ten minutes postscript into a six hour political and economic lecture, and if they wrote letters, many of which I am afraid are still strewn all up and down the country, to which they expected a reply; and thanks—well, thanks for the thousands of pleasant letters, for all manner of little kindnesses and expressions of gratitude and, for listening. I'll always be proud to remember how many times I caught your ear as we all marched through the blitzkrieg together. It might have been worse, mightn't it?